A Land Without Time

A Land Without Time

A Peace Corps Volunteer in Afghanistan

John Sumser

Published in 2006 by
Academy Chicago Publishers
363 West Erie Street
Chicago, Illinois 60610

Printed and bound in the U.S.A.

Library of Congress Cataloging-in-Publication Data on file with the publisher

This is for
Chuck, Ed, Jessie, Melissa and
all Peace Corps volunteers, past and present.

It's been almost three decades since the events described in this book took place, but the book itself began only a few years ago at a party when Nanette Asimov, a reporter for the *San Francisco Chronicle*, suggested that I write down a story I had told her over dinner. I would like to thank Nanette for her suggestion, all my friends and students for listening to these stories for so many years, my agent Sally Hill McMillan for all of her efforts and, of course, Jordan Miller, Sarah Olson and the whole team at Academy Chicago for helping me put out such a beautiful book. I would also like to thank my wife, Helen, for all of her help, and my children, Tim and Laura, for putting up with me.

CONTENTS

KABUL, THE SECOND TIME

THE LAST DAYS

INTRODUCTION

EVERY PLACE MENTIONED IN THIS BOOK IS GONE. I HAVE SEEN a lot of photographs of Afghanistan recently, and the places where I have been and where I have lived are unrecognizable. The homes, schools, stores, and government offices could have been reduced to rubble by the Soviet Union or the United States, by the Taliban or the Northern Coalition, or simply by earthquakes . . . not even God wanting to be left out of the frenzy of destruction. The photos show us that there is almost nothing left of this country, making it hard to imagine that there ever was anything before this period of pale brown destruction and thin-fingered desperation.

There was a time not so long ago when Afghanistan was just another obscure part of the world; a dusty, lumpy patch of rocky land which kept Pakistan from collapsing into Iran. When news of my arrest as a spy was reported in the *San Jose Mercury-News* thirty years ago, the headline shouted "San Josean Seized as Spy in African Coup." Today everyone knows Afghanistan is not in Africa, but I am afraid that *Afghanistan* is becoming less the name of a place and more the name of a war . . . or of a part of a war. Or maybe just a part of a problem: a pawn, as the British would have put it a hundred years ago, in the Great Game of international politics. It may be that, like Vietnam, its identity will be collapsed into something having to do with the interests and actions of the United States rather than anything intrinsic to the people who lived there, eking out their meager livings in the arid, narrow valleys. Perhaps, as Berlin once symbolized the war be-

tween Capitalism and Communism, Kabul will come to symbol-
ize the war between the Developed and the Undeveloped nations.
The place itself will be overlooked.

This is something that should not happen.

Afghanistan has always been the space between countries. It
is as if all those neatly outlined patches of colors on the maps
shrank just a bit and the edges pulled away from each other at this
particularly tricky juncture; its shape too ungainly, its surface too
uneven for the edges to hold. The Chinese, Iranians, and Indians
have dominated the land that Afghanistan occupies. Geography,
language, and culture have always divided it. The Russians, the
British, the Mongols, and the Greeks have invaded its territory. It
was Afghanistan that marked the outward progress of Alexander
the Great. It was in Afghanistan that Tamerlain was lamed. It was
in Afghanistan that the British and Russian armies failed, wither-
ing in the tortuous terrain.

Now the Americans are there, setting up bases in Kandahar and
making sorties into the Hindu Kush. And the journalists are hitch-
ing rides with the soldiers, earning their red badges and hoping
for advancement, sending home pictures of desolation and exotic
incompetence. The constant stream of news stories is converting
the country into an issue, a problem, a piece of a puzzle, but the
journalists are already losing interest because, after all, isn't Iran
more interesting? Isn't that today's big story? Or Pakistan?

This book is a small effort to round out the cartoon simplicity
of a disaster area. This is a look at a time spent in Afghanistan
that ended just as the disaster began, with the Communist coup
of 1979. It is the story of the interaction between Americans in
the Peace Corps and the people of Afghanistan. Or at least my
perspective on that interaction. This book tells the story of how I
ended up going to this accidental country almost by chance, how
I learned to live there, and how I got swept up in the coup that
ended up sucking in so many people from so many nations.

GETTING THERE

THE DECISION

IT WAS ANOTHER ASSEMBLY. WE WERE IN THE AUDITORIUM OF a bankrupt college near Putney, Vermont. It was the first week of Peace Corps training and there was an endless number of assemblies. This time, one of the speakers was a guy named Rick, who was trying to get eight volunteers to go to Afghanistan.

I was sitting with a few hundred other people and, like many of them, I was planning on going to Morocco. I was thinking that if I went to Morocco I would meet Ingrid Bergman and see Claude Raines round up the usual suspects. I could picture myself in the airport in Casablanca in the fog, watching airplanes come in suspended by thin strings. Meanwhile, there was this very un-Humphrey-Bogart-looking man telling us about a country called Afghanistan that was in Asia or Africa or someplace. Even worse, directly across the aisle from me was the surly older guy who had been such a jackass the previous evening.

Last night, many of the volunteers had wandered into town and gone into the only bar in Putney. Most of the women who volunteered to go into the Peace Corps were extremely attractive and I was trying to get to know one or two of them. The two I was talking with were amazingly silly and so, being in a bar and on the make, I traded my normal dignity for a beer and was playing along with whatever it was they were doing. A voice abruptly cut into our antics with something like, "If you people are going to be so cheerful, could you take it somewhere else?"

We all turned and found a dour-looking man with thinning hair. He sat there looking as if he had been condemned to occupy the stool, forced against his will to be surrounded by boisterous people. He was about the same age as the rest of us, but his sober seriousness added years to his demeanor. I felt I had to say something, so I said, "Look, old man, if you don't like it here maybe you should leave." It was something like that. It's been twenty years, and I can still remember exactly how it felt. In my memory, there is the blurry image of the two women, and a very clear sense of turning to this guy, calling him an old man, and suggesting that he leave. He had a beer in one hand, a longneck bottle that he was holding with his fingers as if he didn't want to warm it up. He rolled his eyes, took a swig from the bottle, and turned away from us.

Now he was sitting across the aisle from me in the auditorium in Vermont. I caught his eye. Rick was still going on about Afghanistan, how it was a hard country and a true Peace Corps experience. The man from the bar said he didn't want to go there. I must have been really bored, because I leaned over and said, "If you're afraid to go there, just say so."

"I don't see you signing up," he said. And there, of course, he had me. Like him, I could say that I simply didn't want to go to Afghanistan, that it had nothing to do with the bleak picture Rick had painted, but that would make me a loud-mouthed jackass. I had, after all, challenged him in the bar and then again with my remark about him being afraid.

I realized I had cooked my own goose. "Actually," I said, "I'm thinking about going there."

"Right," he snorted. "I'd go if you went."

"Really? Then let's go." This was strange. Our only interaction had been in the bar and now we were planning our future together.

He stared at me for a moment, then said, "You're still sitting down."

So, I stood up to walk down the aisle to volunteer for Afghanistan, wherever the hell that was. I took a step or two then turned and looked back at the man from the bar who was still sitting in his seat. I made chicken noises. I think I had gotten another five feet or so when I heard him stand up and walk down behind me.

Rick was standing behind a podium, on a stage, and there were two or three people waiting to talk to him. Some of them were just asking for information and I briefly thought about only asking a couple of questions, but then I let go of the image of Casablanca, and put my name on the list.

I waited while the man from the bar added his name to the list. He turned and walked over to me. "You know," he said, "you're not exactly a spring chicken yourself."

I must have looked confused because he said, "You called me an old man last night."

"Well, you were acting like some grumpy old man. 'You kids settle down.' You sounded like someone's parent."

"I was in a bad mood and you were acting like an asshole."

"Did you see those two girls?" I asked him.

"Okay" he said, conceding the point. It was probably the only point he ever conceded to me in the time I knew him.

"And besides," I told him, "at least I don't go around saying things like 'spring chicken.'"

Years later, I was doing research on the AIDS epidemic and came to understand what is known as Rational Choice Theory. This is the idea that we make life choices basically the same way we decide which refrigerator we want to buy. It is an academically popular but absolutely ridiculous idea on many levels—and the stories I will tell about my time in the Peace Corps will certainly show this theory has little to say about my decision-making processes—but the image that always pops into my head when I have to teach Rational Choice Theory is of me and the man from the bar walking down to volunteer to go to Afghanistan. Many things could be said about how Chuck Norton and I made that choice, but the word "rational" would probably not be in any of them.

THE GROUP

CHUCK NORTON, THE MAN FROM THE BAR, WAS A FORMER ARMY Ranger, about a year or two older than I was. It was a good thing that I hadn't suggested we take our little bar confrontation outside because he probably could have stuffed me into the beer bottle he was carrying. Or, worse, the opposite. Ed was the youngest in our group. He was a good-looking, personable, generous man. Like Chuck, he was a good athlete. There was a couple, Jim and Betty. Jim had a business degree from one of the state colleges in California. All I remember about Betty is that she had an almost pathological dislike of dirt and bugs, and that she could draw really cute pictures to use as learning props. I think the Peace Corps was Jim's idea. There was a tall thin man named Will, whose main interest in going to Afghanistan seemed to be getting nearer to India. Then there was Jessie and Melissa. Jessie was a tall, strikingly pretty, extremely intelligent and independent woman. One night over beer on the dorm balcony in Vermont—there was a lot of beer in Vermont, it seems—some of the men were trying to figure out who the three most attractive volunteers were and everyone agreed that she was one of them. I told Jessie that later, in Afghanistan, but I don't think she believed me. Then there was Melissa.

I met Melissa in Hartford, Connecticut, at the bus station. We all had instructions: get to Hartford, take a Peter Pan bus to Putney, Vermont. I thought it odd that I had to fly to one state to get to another, but New England is like that. Melissa was destined

to carry the burden of being the prettiest woman in Kabul, but
that morning she was just a slightly harried, somewhat nervous
volunteer wondering if she was standing in the right place to catch
a Peter Pan bus to Vermont. (She may have been wondering, like
me, if the directions for the bus to Vermont were "second star to
the right and straight on 'til morning.")

I lost track of Melissa after leaving Afghanistan. For a while,
she was in South America with a Frenchman she married. Then
she was in France. Then in India. And, wherever she is now, if you
look closely at her chin you will see a very small scar that she got
while waiting for the bus in Hartford. She was bent over, trying to
bungie-cord her suitcases to a small, and I think broken, suitcase
caddie. The cord whipped up and the hook end caught her right
under her chin. Melissa was not having a good day.

She also had way too much stuff and looked way over-dressed.
She was perfectly made up, her luggage matched, her outfit was
stylish. I remember thinking two things: one, that I should have
gotten a haircut before leaving and, two, one of us was going to
be really out of place. What I didn't know, at the time, was that
the bungie cord hit her hard enough to leave a scar. Melissa was
much tougher than she looked.

I don't remember much about Peace Corps training. I know we
learned more about breast feeding in Africa than anyone needed to
know. After a couple of weeks, we all started skipping the breast-
feeding lectures on the grounds that we would be killed if we talked
to Afghan women about their breasts. We studied Farsi every minute
when we were not learning about breast feeding, teaching courses
to French-speaking Canadian teenagers, or waiting in line to get
shots. We took courses in teaching English as a Second Language
and had to watch a professor from Dartmouth named Rassias make
an absolute fool of himself. He yelled and bounced around, threw
chairs, and ripped open his shirt. "That," someone whispered to me,
"would work really well in a rural Muslim schoolroom."

We got shots for everything, including rabies. One of the shot series resulted in all of us getting the giggles and that was the only day in which the rest of the schedule was canceled. I remember dozens of us sprawled on the lawn that afternoon, talking aimlessly and laughing about almost everything.

I had a roommate who could not seem to learn anything. About the sixth week of super-intensive French lessons, he asked me which word was the verb in "*Je suis étudiant.*" The next day, he was given an assignment planting trees on some tropical English-speaking island. I remember standing on the balcony at the end of the dorm. He took a photo of me with a wonderful woman who was going to the Upper Volta and never sent it to me. He said I could buy it from him. The woman and I talked about how we were going to the two countries vying for the shortest life expectancies while he was going to plant trees in the Caribbean. She and I promised to write to each other and neither of us did.

———

The problem was that the airport in Tehran was called an international airport. JFK is an international airport. So is LAX and SFO and O'Hare. DeGaulle. Heathrow. Lots of names come to mind, and with the names come certain expectations. We were all a little nervous about getting to Afghanistan and so the layover in Iran was welcomed. We would be in an exotic locale, but in the capital of an oil-rich nation, so we saw it—or at least I saw it—as a bridging experience: a safe place, vaguely familiar, somewhere between here and there. We would be in familiar territory: an International Airport.

But Tehran International Airport was a little different. It was much closer to there than to here. The food, for example, was all theirs and the smell of the cooking filled the lobby. This was a confusing experience for me: on the one hand, I had an opportunity to try very different food in a relatively clean environment. On the other hand, I was in an airport and airport food is almost never any good. I compromised and nibbled at kabobs and other things that looked recognizable. Jim and Betty, much to my surprise, jumped right in and were trying almost everything.

The Peace Corps, being a government agency, had screwed up and given us vouchers for four hotel rooms, but only enough money for one cab. It was late evening and we were scheduled to fly out early the next morning. We discussed the situation and decided that Melissa and Jessie, and Jim and Betty should take the cab to the hotel. Ed, Chuck, Will, and I would just hang out at the airport. The ride to the hotel was close to an hour and it seemed like an awful lot of trouble in order to get four or five hours sleep, especially after having dozed for hours on the flight from New York. The airport was probably the liveliest part of Iran at 11:00 at night, so volunteering to forgo the hotel was not a huge sacrifice.

We stayed in a loose group, each of us breaking away to wander around on our own. Chuck and Ed came up to me at one point, each holding plates of food.

"Guess what?" Ed asked. "We don't know the names of anything to eat."

"So how did you get that stuff?"

"Eee ba Farsi ch'eese," Chuck said and we all laughed. It used to drive our teacher crazy that, no matter know much we learned, we never evolved beyond "What is this in Farsi?" But we learned in the course of an hour or so that we could, in fact survive, at least if we stayed in international airports and had some spending money. This was a valuable lesson. We confirmed that we weren't going to be overwhelmed by the mere fact that we were in South Central Asia and that we had learned how to speak rudimentary Farsi.

The biggest shock was the bathroom. We had been told about toilets in this part of the world, but we didn't expect to see them at the airport. Walking into the restroom at Tehran International Airport was pretty much like walking into any restroom in any airport, until you actually entered a stall. Inside the stall was a shallow porcelain tray with a hole in the center. On each side of the hole were raised footprints with ridges; a safety feature should they happen to become wet, which of course they always were. The footprints were facing forward, so you were required to step backward on to them, taking care that none of your clothing actually touched the tray-toilet. Once settled, you started to think *This isn't so bad*, until you took the time to look around the stall. That's when you noticed there wasn't any toilet paper. Instead, there was a plastic pitcher of water. I remembered one of the instructors in Vermont talking about this.

When learning the social taboos of Afghanistan we were told that you don't show the bottom of your feet to anyone, that you don't make the "okay" circle with your thumb and forefinger, and that you never, ever, offer or accept anything using your left hand. After using the toilet, you were expected to pour water from the pitcher into your left hand and then use your left hand to clean the area normally attacked with wads of toilet paper. The problem, for Americans, was that after you did this, you immediately looked around for some toilet paper because now your bottom was all wet. After Tehran, we all carried toilet paper wherever we went.

The next morning we boarded the Ariana Airlines flight to Kabul. (Ariana is the ancient name for Afghanistan.) It was a small jet, two seats on each side of the isle. Chuck and I were sitting on the right side of the plane, close to the bulkhead that formed the kitchen. The plane started to push back and then everyone started yelling because the forward passenger door hadn't been closed. The plane came to a halt and the stewardess carried on a conversation with one of the ground crew. We had moved too far from the platform for someone from outside to close the door, so we either had to move forward or try to close it from inside.

The stewardess gave it a try, leaning way out of the plane and trying to swing the door out from the plane and into the doorway. She wasn't strong enough, so she asked the pilot to help. Chuck and I volunteered to help, but the stewardess told us to stay in our seats. We watched the pilot and the stewardess try to get the door closed.

Next time you board a plane, take a look at the door and imagine trying to close it from inside. The door opened straight out and then swung to one side so that it was flush with the fuselage of the plane. Somehow, the two crew members managed to rock the door away from the fuselage and then pull it closed. In doing so, however, the heavy door gained quite a lot of momentum and, while the stewardess managed to get out of the way, the door smacked the pilot in the head, knocking him across the aisle and into the kitchen bulkhead. He bounced off the bulkhead and fell to the floor.

Chuck looked at me. "Not a good sign."

The pilot staggered to his feet and went back into the flight deck. There was a slight wobble in his walk.

A few minutes later, we pushed back, and not long after that we took off on the last leg of our journey to Afghanistan.

KABUL, THE FIRST TIME

RED PANTS

THE DECISION ABOUT THE PANTS IS DIFFICULT TO RECONSTRUCT.
I had to decide what I was going to pack, what I was going to carry on the airplane, and what I was going to wear. It would take two days to get to Afghanistan: New York to Bonn, then Bonn to Tehran, where we would spend the night. The following day we would fly from Tehran to Kabul. Following some perverse reasoning process, I decided that I would wear my least favorite clothes. Perhaps I was thinking that it didn't matter very much how one looked on an airplane or in various airports.

I had an almost brand-new pair of red corduroy pants. I have no idea why I ever bought them, but it was the late 1970s, a time that is virtually incomprehensible from this vantage point. I may have received the pants as a Christmas gift. I hope I received them as a Christmas gift. (Actually, in the process of writing this, I have decided to have clear memories of getting them as a gift, thus absolving myself of all responsibility.)

Looking back, it seems impossible that the Peace Corps let us bring the motley collection of junk that many of us brought. Certainly, if I were heading off to spend two years in Afghanistan today, I would bring very different sorts of things. I would bring good camping gear, quality outdoor clothing, water-filter kits. REI, Northface, and L.L. Bean would love to provide my equipment and supplies.

But I was dirt-poor in those days. I knew I would be away from a dentist for two years, so I had spent almost all of my money having my teeth fixed. I brought the clothes I had worn as a college student in San Jose, California. And I also brought the red pants that I didn't wear as a college student, but that were in my closet, tempting in their shiny newness. We were told to bring a spare pair of glasses, so I brought a pair with a prescription that was three or four years out of date. They were broken when my suitcase was dented by the airlines. The lack of a backup pair of glasses became a problem when my real glasses were stolen by a woman who, as far as I could tell, had been offended by my nudity when she walked in and caught me showering in the men's dorm bathroom in Vermont.

God knows what she would have taken if she had caught me showering in the women's bathroom.

So I carefully packed away all the clothes that I considered better than my red pants and checked the bag safely in the belly of the airplane. The suitcase was, as far as I could tell, used by the airlines in their training courses on things not to do with suitcases. That, at least, is what I concluded when it landed in Kabul three weeks after I did, held together with packing tape.

But I arrived in Kabul wearing red pants. I wore red pants every day for three weeks. Fortunately, it was summer and relentlessly hot, so I didn't have to sleep in the damn things.

One day in the Peace Corps office, near the mailboxes, an older volunteer sidled up to me.

"Hey," he said, and introduced himself.

We talked a while; this and that, where are you from, where are you working.

"You know," he said. "I can lend you some clothes."

"Ah, that's nice of you, but I'm okay."

"But you wear the same clothes every day."

I found the whole clothing thing embarrassing and had been working on the premise that no one had noticed I was wearing red pants and a blue denim shirt every day. "Nah, it's okay. I called the airline and my luggage should be here any day now."

"Any day now." He let the phrase hang there in its own little vacuum.

"Yeah." It was stupid, but I pretended I believed it. I was getting tired of walking up the long hill to the Inter-Continental Hotel where the airline office was located. They hated seeing me coming. "They told me that they found the bags."

"Really."

"Yeah." Surely this guy would go away soon.

"I heard some of the girls talking," he said. "They called you the 'guy with the red pants.'"

"Really?" This wasn't good news. I had already been warned that my chances of getting laid while in Afghanistan were very low and I had assumed that calculation was based on the idea that I was perceived to be reasonably normal.

He nodded, very seriously. "Yeah. I acted like I didn't know who they were talking about and asked, 'Who you guys talking about? What's his name?' And the girls said they didn't know your name."

"Really?" Shit.

He mimicked a falsetto, "You know, the guy with the red pants."

"Wow."

"So, you want to borrow some clothes until you get your stuff?"

"Yeah. That would be really cool."

About two days later, my baggage arrived and I threw the red pants away.

———

I had been warned about not getting laid as I stepped off the airplane in Kabul. Two volunteers met us and before both feet were on Afghan soil (or, at least, Afghan tarmac), one of them said to us, "You may think you are going to get laid here, but it's not going to happen."

Chuck looked at me. I told him I had heard guys in Los Angeles say the same thing.

These were two funny men, though. Tony and Danny were

part of a group that had received training in Afghanistan while the rest of us were trained in Vermont, so we were roughly equal in academic understanding, but they had more direct experience. One day, sitting in the shade at the Peace Corps office during a language lesson, we had to mention things we loved. The teacher—an Afghan man—expected to go around the circle getting responses like "I love ice cream" or "I love my girlfriend," "I love Kabul in the spring time." That sort of thing. When it was his turn, Danny said, "I love my hand."

The teacher shook his head, thinking Danny had misused a word, but Danny insisted that he loved his hand. When the teacher finally understood what he meant, he turned bright red.

Danny was from New York City. He wanted to be a writer.

"So you're going to write about Afghanistan?" I asked him.

"No. I'm writing a novel about living in New York." I thought at the time that was really odd to go so far away in order to write about home, but now I am at home writing about Afghanistan.

There was another volunteer from New York, an African-American woman who left before finishing her training. Afghans refused to believe she came from the United States and as a result she was treated quite badly. She was also extremely afraid of Afghanistan. It got to the point where she was afraid to walk around the city. I remember asking her how she could grow up in the Bronx and be afraid of Afghanistan. Afghanistan, at that time, was the least violent place I had ever been. I have no idea how much real danger she was in, but Afghanistan through the eyes of a fairly gutsy African-American woman was apparently a very frightening place. The Peace Corps was a very white institution, at least when I was in, so it was sad when she left.

———

One of the things we had to do almost immediately was to get Afghan identification cards made. During my stay in Afghanistan, no one ever asked to see my card: identification cards in a land with a 95% illiteracy rate are meaningless. Societies that operate on the presumption of illiteracy are not as obsessed with paper as we are. Chuck, Ed, Melissa, Jessie, Jim, Betty, and I went to a small photography shop to have our pictures taken. The shop had two rooms divided by a heavy black curtain; a waiting room with a clerk behind a desk and the room where the photographer worked. We crowded into the tiny waiting room and Chuck was the first called to go into the second room to get his photograph taken.

Chuck was laughing when he pushed his way past the curtain to come back into the waiting room.

"What's so funny?"

"You'll see," he said.

Ed went next and he shook his head in mock amazement when he came back into the waiting room. "Don't say anything!" Chuck warned him. "Let them see for themselves."

Then it was my turn. Past the curtain was a room with the walls painted black. A large varnished box on a tripod stood on one side of the room facing a stool about four feet away. I sat on the stool and the cameraman moved me around so that I was in the proper position, then went over to the large box camera. The camera was made of wood and was at least a foot square. A capped lens was stuck in the middle of the side facing me. The photographer looked from me to the lens a few times to make sure we were lined up. He adjusted one of the lights. Then he reached over and snatched the cap off the lens, waited a second or two, and quickly replaced it.

And he told me I was finished.

None of us could believe that the photos would come out well. An American photographer would have taken two or three pictures just to make sure that one was good. An American photographer would have used a high-tech Japanese camera with an 80-millimeter lens and would know all about aperture and shutter-speed adjustments. This man had a wooden box apparently stolen from an American Civil War museum and his shutter speed adjustments took place in his brain and his wrist. There was no aperture adjustment, just a hole in the side of the box.

When the IDs arrived, the photographs were better than the ones on our passports.

This was my first lesson in how much—and how well—you could do with very little. Afghans were masters at exhausting the potential of whatever scarce resources were available.

PILSNER URQUEL

THE MIAMI CAFE SERVED FANTASTIC WIENER SCHNITZEL. IT WAS thin, crusty and yet managed to be moist and tender. Once in a while, it was really good to eat Western food. I would go to the Miami, which was about halfway between the Peace Corps office and Chicken Street, to get two orders of schnitzel and two Fantas. I'd take the food outside where I'd sit on the rooftop patio and swoon with culinary pleasure.

I always needed two Fantas: one to quench my thirst and one to drink with the meal(s). Fanta was better than Coca-Cola, because Fanta was almost non-carbonated which made it possible to guzzle without getting a stomach full of gas. I needed two orders of schnitzel because I was always famished. I think the average male volunteer in Afghanistan weighed twenty or thirty pounds less than in the States and was always hungry. It was one of the reasons we were so rarely invited to diplomatic parties: We would descend like locusts, leaving refrigerators (yes! refrigerators!) and larders bare. (The women volunteers, in contrast, tended to gain weight. The theory was that men lost weight because there was no beer and women gained weight because they ate when they were depressed.)

One afternoon, around one or two o'clock, I went to the Miami. After eating my two meals and drinking one of my Fantas, I sat writing a letter at my table on the patio.

"Excuse me," someone called.

I looked up. A man I hadn't noticed was sitting at a table in the shade cast by the outside wall of the restaurant. I didn't know him. I said hello.

"You are an American," he asked. He spoke with the lilt of an Indian, which renders question marks unnecessary.

"Yes," I said. "And you are from India?" As an American, I had trouble asking if he was an Indian. Indians, for me, are bundled up with that whole teepee-buffalo thing.

"I knew you were an American because you are drinking soda."

"Ah." I never drank soda in the United States. I drank soda in Afghanistan because I couldn't drink the water.

"Come sit with me."

A little odd. This struck me as a slightly off-center, like a pick-up. Could I get picked up by an Indian man in a restaurant in Kabul? Probably. I turned over this proposition. Middle of the afternoon. Nothing much going on and the whole point of being in this country was to talk to people I otherwise would never meet. On the other hand, this really felt odd to me.

"I should finish this letter," I said. I waved at the letter, pen in hand, so that he could see I was busy.

"I want to buy you a beer," he told me. "You are too old to be drinking that orange stuff."

A beer. I couldn't afford to buy beer. I didn't even know that the Miami sold beer. A gay Indian—how awkward could it get? I grew up in Los Angeles so I knew how to diffuse sexually ambiguous situations. I put my stuff away and went over to his table. We shook hands and introduced ourselves.

"I will get you a Pilsner Urquel," he said. "Have you had this before?" He was a short man, somewhat overweight, with a round happy face. He was perhaps thirty or thirty-five.

I told him I hadn't had Pilsner Urquel before and he shook his head in dismay. This, he seemed to say, was what he expected of an American, a grown man who drank soft drinks in the midday sun. "Then you must try it. I have had the American Budweiser and it is not beer. It has no taste."

Years later, a French friend of mine told me that in France you walk off the beach and are immediately surrounded by culture, but in America—specifically, San Diego—you are surrounded by nothing: fast food, chain restaurants and stores, malls. You are surrounded, I told him, by American culture: Why would you expect to walk off the beach in San Diego and end up in Juan-les-Pins? Budweiser tastes like American beer because it is made in America.

A few months after this lunch at the Miami, while I was at an embassy party, an Englishman told me that bourbon wasn't whiskey. I showed him the bottle and pointed out that the label said bourbon whiskey. Only scotch, he told me, and Irish whiskeys are whiskeys. Bourbon is some sort of Colonial beverage, a cheap imitation.

Americans travel to broaden their perspectives and run smack into European provincialism wherever they go.

The man from India poured the beer into my glass for me, thinking perhaps, that otherwise I would look around for a straw.

"Taste it," he said, pushing the glass across the table.

I did. I did again. "This is really good beer," I told him.

One of the things I made a point of doing when I got back to the U.S. was to buy Pilsner Urquel for all of my friends.

He was a rug merchant, the Indian, and told me stories of his travels through small villages in Afghanistan. We finished the beers and he ordered another round. Then another round. The sun sparkled off the windows across the road and heat built in waves from the rooftop while we sat in the shade, telling stories for hours.

After my third beer (his fourth) we realized we would either have to stop or commit ourselves to getting smashed in the middle of the afternoon. The conversation slowly wound down until we sat in silence, staring across the rooftops.

"You have a letter to write, I think," he said.

"Yes, I do. And you have rugs to buy." I shuffled around in my chair, miming leaving. He stood up. I joined him and the sun hit me in the head like a sledgehammer.

"It was good talking," he told me. "Most Americans take one look at me and think, 'He doesn't speak English.'"

"Really? I thought most people in India spoke English."

"We do," he said. "We speak English better than Americans."

Of course you do.

BOLTING CUPS TOGETHER

MOST SHOPS IN AFGHANISTAN ARE MORE LIKE KIOSKS THAN stores. Usually, you walked up to a counter and spoke with the shopkeeper, who got what you wanted from one of the shelves behind the counter. Generally, there were lots of things piled in front of the counter as well as on top of the counter, so you had to be careful not to step on things or bump merchandise off the counter. Quite often the shopkeeper was around twelve years old.

The boy who ran the shop around the corner from the Peace Corps temporary housing was busy tearing up magazines when I went to buy some cigarettes. It was mid-morning and just beginning to warm up. He was working his way through a copy of *Der Spiegel*, quickly tearing out each page and putting it on top of a rather large stack of pages on the table behind the counter.

"What are you doing?" I asked him. He didn't understand the question. "Why are you tearing the paper?" I didn't know the words for magazine or for page.

His face lit up. "I'm making bags."

"How do you make a bag out of that paper?"

He stood up and put a sheet of paper on the counter. It was an ad of some sort, scotch or cigarettes. He did something magical with his hands, brushed on some paste, and there was a small paper sack.

I laughed. "Slower," I said. "I couldn't see."

He slowed down and was careful to keep his hands out of the way, so that I could see. He was a kid, not yet a teenager, and he

was a little confused that he had to show me something so obvious. He was making small bags for loose spices and candies.

I thanked him. I thought of all the bags that I threw away
when I was home. I thought of America: Man! Could we make
bags! We make shopping bags for regular plain-folks markets and
shopping bags with handles for fancy markets, and then there are
all those Macy's and Nordstrom bags. We have special bags for
ice cream and we have paper or plastic? We don't make silly-ass
bags with German advertisements on them . . . although some
boutique owner may read this and have some whipped up. We
made great bags, but I couldn't make a bag at all. And none of my
friends could make one either, as far as I knew. Yet up and down
this street, and all across this country, boys and men were tearing
up yesterday's stories of *earthshaking events* and turning them
into thousands of small bags for loose items.

Just behind this store was a small workshop where men made
utensils and cookware out of old ghee cans. Ghee is a lard-like
substance imported from India. It's clarified butter, I've been told,
although I am not quite sure what that means. Afghans use it in all
of their restaurant cooking. The favorite restaurant in Kabul for
breakfast—at least among the Peace Corps volunteers, although we
were repeatedly warned away from it for health reasons—would
serve eggs literally floating in a pond of ghee. Chuck used to shout,
"More ghee! We need more ghee!" and they would slop some more
onto his plate. It came in five-gallon cans that the workshop men
shaped into cups, pots, pans, ladles, and canisters.

Jim, of Jim and Betty, was working for the Ministry of the Interior. Jim was perhaps the most valuable member of our cohort.
He was solid, unflappable, knowledgeable, and ultimately had to
go home because his wife was being driven insane by the flies. We
watched her lose it over the course of a month. She had a pathological aversion to flies and yet tried to stick it out for Jim's sake.
It was horrible to watch her try to eat.

I remember watching her waving the flies away as she tried to
protect her food, yelling at the flies, and on the verge of tears. I
remarked to another volunteer that it made sense to hate flies in

the United States, but no sense to hate flies here, where they were so thick you could actually breathe them in while walking. Flies in the U.S., I thought, were an avoidable annoyance. Flies in Afghanistan were absolutely unavoidable during the summer. The other volunteer didn't agree. "It makes perfect sense," he said. "Flies in the U.S. are only theoretically disgusting. Flies here can kill you."

Yeah, there was that.

But Jim didn't seem to mind the flies. And, as part of his job at the Ministry of the Interior, he was given a tour of some of the government's warehouses in Kabul. In the warehouses, he told us, there were bins that were simply enormous. You had to climb tall ladders to be able to see into them. And in the bins were all the dried-up pens from all the government offices. There were bins with dead batteries and old typewriter ribbons. There was a bin, he said, full of springs of different sizes.

It was funny listening to him talk. It was as if he had gotten to see another dimension in a parallel universe. His eyes would be big with memory and he would speak in a tone of amazed respect. He really thought that everything that had ever broken or worn out in Afghanistan had been carefully saved, in case there might be a need for it in the future. Or maybe not even that, because he couldn't find out exactly why they were saving the old pens. Maybe they stored these things because the idea of simply throwing something away made so little sense that there weren't even places in which you could throw things.

When you travel in rural areas in the United States, it seems that every household is surrounded by its own personal garbage dump. There are huge piles of rusting equipment, weed-filled vehicles, crippled furniture, and trash. But in Afghanistan, they have very little of anything, so they waste very little of anything. They took Europe's cast-off clothing and worn-out trucks and put them to use well beyond their commercially-expected lifespans.

They always made me feel wasteful. I felt as though I ate too much and talked too loudly. I had almost nothing by American standards, but I had far too much for one person living in Afghanistan.

Simply being able to be one person, living in Afghanistan, was a luxury beyond the imagination of most of the people I met. I wasted most of the space in the apartment I rented. Why would any one person need four rooms?

CORRUPTING THE CULTURE

ONE OF THE THINGS WE TALKED ABOUT QUITE A BIT, ESPECIALLY in the beginning, was our relationship to the Afghan people and the Afghan culture. On the one hand, we were supposed to help the Afghans reach goals that were largely, if not entirely, determined by the Afghans themselves. We would nudge, of course, and suggest family planning or winter wheat, but by and large, we were not supposed to be a culturally-destructive influence. On the other hand, our mere presence was destructive. Or, at least, insidious. We were, for example, from a Christian culture, which shaped us regardless of our personal beliefs. We were also from a culture that allowed women roughly the same opportunities as men. We were individualists while Afghans were collectivists. We represented wealth to them and they represented poverty to us. We were cosmopolitan; they were provincial. We were secular, they were religious.

For a Peace Corps volunteer to stand on the street corner, doing nothing, his hands in his pockets, was to erode Afghan society. It was difficult to imagine anything more American, and less Afghan, than a Peace Corps volunteer. That's one of the reasons volunteers were suspect. It made no sense to many of the Afghans I talked with that someone would leave the United States in order to live in Afghanistan, especially if the Americans weren't being paid very much money. It was widely assumed that we were either being paid substantial amounts of money that we were choosing not to spend or that we had ulterior motives, like spying.

We were new in the country, so we fluctuated wildly between finding everything in Afghanistan completely wonderful, and seeing almost everything as being in need of some serious re-thinking. And we also saw ourselves in opposition to how we saw the country, so that when we found the place wonderful, we seriously questioned the legitimacy of what we were doing. When we found the place inherently flawed, we considered ourselves quite useful.

Once evening, Chuck, Ed, Will, and I dropped in on Melissa and Jessie. We drank tea and argued about the role of the Peace Corps. Will, surprisingly enough given his spiritual nature, really didn't give a damn about the Afghans, or the Indians, or the Pakistanis. He had a naive belief in karma that translated into a sort of Calvinistic version of Hinduism, which was that everyone is going to get what they are going to get and there was no sense trying to change anything. He coupled this with the belief that no earthly condition could be said to be either good or bad, that I would imagine was a ploy designed to keep Calvinists of all stripes from being either overwhelmed by guilt or driven insane.

The conversation was typical at first: was SONY really going to set up a broadcast network? Were the Afghans correct in keeping out Christian missionaries?

Would dropping cheap watches all over the country completely destroy the culture?

We were sitting on the floor because there was no furniture in the room. Will was leaning against the wall and I was facing him. He and I got into one of those heated arguments that only men in their twenties can get into, where the longer you argue, the further apart you get, until no one is anywhere near their normally held beliefs and the other person is the Anti-Christ. Melissa and Jessie got tired of listening to us and went to bed. The argument ended when Will began explaining how no one could say that Hitler was a really bad fellow and I threw the cold remnants of my tea in his face. I wanted him to get up so that I could beat the shit out him, but since no earthly condition was inherently good or bad, he wasn't that bothered by having tea thrown in his face. It was simply another thing that occurred on the planet earth.

Jessie, on the other hand, jumped out of bed wearing only a t-shirt, panties, and the longest legs I had seen at that point in my life, threw on a pair of shorts and ran out into the living room. Her living room, I remembered. She kicked us out, saying she was trying to sleep and we were all acting like idiots.

We piled out of her apartment, and wandered off to our various residences. Chuck and I walked together.

Chuck said he knew I was going to throw the tea. He could see it coming.

"It seemed so British," I said, "and corny. But I was furious and didn't know what else to do."

"He would have kicked your ass if he'd gotten up," Chuck told me.

"I don't think so."

"He's quite an athlete."

"I wasn't worried," I said. "Did you see Jessie's legs when she got out of bed?"

"No. She was wearing shorts."

"Not when she was in bed," I said. "She jumped out wearing a t-shirt and underwear, and then put the shorts on."

"Really?" he asked. "I'll tell her that I saw her underwear."

And he did, the next day. He was incorrigible.

But the question of our role in the country was always something we were at least dimly aware of, like background music or white noise. Chuck and I talked about becoming Peace Corps Bums, an altruistic version of beach bums, but with roughly the same lifestyle. After Afghanistan, we'd go somewhere else, and then somewhere else. We would drift around the planet under the guise of doing good to the downtrodden, and spend out lives hanging out with interesting people in interesting places.

It was a flippant rationale for our presence, but relatively honest. The contradiction between our values and our presence was so great that some flippancy was required. Afghanistan, we knew, was a country you could drown in, overwhelmed by the sounds, smells, and sights, and by the staggering geography and the endless history. And we were there to move them one or two steps closer to suburban America. Good steps, there was no question, and innocuous in themselves, but subversive.

———————

Marty, the Assistant Director of the Peace Corps in Afghanistan, called a meeting to talk about our assignments. Almost everyone wanted to stay in Kabul, but Marty told us there were two sites outside the capital. There was an opening in Kandahar for one person and two positions available in Laghman Province.

"Do they speak Farsi in Kandahar?" Jessie asked. We knew Kandahar was in the far south of the country.

"Yeah, but they also speak Pushtun."

"How close is that to Farsi?"

"It's a different language," we were told, "not just a dialect."

If you look at a map of South Central Asia, you'll see that Afghanistan is a landlocked nation. Iran and Pakistan meet south of Afghanistan, cutting it off from the Indian Ocean. The southern part of Afghanistan, as well as the Iran-Pakistan corridor, is ethnically Pushtun. The Iran-Afghan-India borders (Pakistan was not yet established) were borders forced on the Afghans by the British, in their typically clumsy Colonial effort that ignored all interests but their own. If the Afghans hadn't successfully fought off repeated British military campaigns, Afghanistan would have been folded into India, then subsequently dissolved into Pakistan. It would have disappeared, as Pushtunistan disappeared. (Istan, as you've probably noticed, means "land of." The Afghans I talked to typically referred to England as "Englistan.")

So Marty was offering Kandahar, and Jessie looked like she was biting. I felt incompetent in Farsi and the idea of learning yet another new language didn't appeal to me. I asked about the other site.

"It's in Laghman," he said. "There are two positions, one in the grammar school and one in the high school."

"Where's Laghman?"

Laghman was east and slightly north of Kabul. It was on the road to Pakistan and occupied the southern part of what used to be Nuristan (land of the light). Nuristanis were reputed to be the remnants of Alexander's army and Nuristanis certainly look different. They have brownish hair and blue eyes, many are freckled and they are much taller than the Afghans in Kabul. The felt, flat-topped hats now associated with Afghan rebels were called Nuristani hats and worn only by Nuristanis and by tourists. You could always spot a Nuristani walking through Kabul because they were so tall, wore hats rather than turbans, and almost always had huge mastiffs on very short leashes.

"Well," I said, "I would like to go there, but there are two positions and Chuck is probably afraid to go outside the big city."

"I'm not afraid," he said. "I just want to think about it. Staying in Kabul sounds like more fun."

"Sure," I said, nodding seriously. "It's okay to stay here where it's easier."

"Do you want to go look at Laghman?" Marty asked Chuck.

"I do," I jumped in, "but Chuck should probably stay here."

"I'll go," Chuck said. "But just to check it out."

And so we went, just to check it out.

It turned out that Melissa, Ed, Jessie and I had already been there. We had gone on a two-day trip into the country and had stopped in Laghman. Melissa and Ed had gone on to Jalalabad while Jessie and I stayed in Laghman.

I don't know if Chuck was afraid, but I know that the idea of being out here by my (Western) self was a little unnerving. Even with Chuck, there would be a sense of isolation that I imagined could be overwhelming. On the other hand, I had opted for Afghanistan because it had occurred to me that if Morocco was exotic, then Afghanistan would be another planet. Following the same train of thought, if Kabul was an adventure, what would this be? Laghman would be worth doing precisely because I would be in so far over my head that I really wondered if I could do it.

The road back to the highway was across a barren flat. The road dipped periodically into gullies. Marty said that this allowed the water from the flash floods to pass over the road without destroying it. Bridges, he said, were always washed away. One of the interesting things I would learn about Afghans was how they could have such clever solutions to some problems and not even see other problems at all.

Marty asked us if we wanted to take the positions in Laghman and we said yes. We had no idea what we were getting into.

LAGHMAN

WATERMELONS

not a town Mehtarlam

LIKE MOST AFGHAN TOWNS, LAGHMAN WAS EXTRAORDINARILY UGLY.
In the middle of the twentieth century, forward-thinking urban planners in Santa Clara, California decided to get rid of all the old buildings and make a modern city. The result, of course, was that they destroyed whatever charm and character there had been and replaced it with strip malls and a government center that looked like a hospital. I think these planners had then been banished to Afghanistan where, full of enthusiasm and devoid of ideas, they created towns that resembled mini-storage facilities.

A lot of the smaller towns and cities in Afghanistan looked as if they were occupied, rather than created, by Afghans. I think, in retrospect, the towns were built by the Soviets or by people influenced by the Soviets. They had a sameness about them that suggested centralized frugality and a complete lack of aesthetic sensibility.

The things that I knew were created by Afghans were not at all like this. The used Bedford trucks, which were the dominant form of transportation when I was there, were repainted by the Afghans in dazzling primary colors. They were bright, garish things festooned with doodads and fringes until they looked like a cross between circus trucks and the cars of Los Angeles low-riders. The shop signs were also painted like this, helped by the fact that Arabic script lends itself to bold, graffiti-like presentations. Afghans made toys and children's furniture that were multi-colored and cheerful. They are famous for their bright red hand-woven rugs.

Important Afghan men wore long, elaborately embroidered coats flung over their shoulders (the sleeves were so long, they were only symbolic). The Afghans had created a culture in sharp contrast to the unrelenting light browns of their environment. And now they did their best to liven up the bland cement-gray of their towns.

Chuck Norton and I rented a house just off the main square of Laghman, which was occupied by a hotel with loudspeakers blaring from each corner. We unloaded our small collection of junk and when we were finished, the place looked really pathetic. We put a striped rug on the dirt floor of the single room and had thrown our cotton-stuffed mattresses on top of it. We had a stove made out of sheet metal that had been one of the recommended purchases. It was completely unusable: we learned that when you start a fire in a sheet-tin box, the entire box becomes red-hot and the rivets pop and you end up with something that looks like modern sculpture. I can't imagine that anyone in the Peace Corps had ever actually used most of the crap that we had wasted our settling-in allowance on.

Kay, the nurse, had brought us down here in the Peace Corps Toyota, and now she was gone. Norton and I looked through the Peace Corps supplies she had given us: iodine tablets for water purification, salt pills, bandages, ointments, condoms.

Norton held up a strip of condoms. "Do you think this will be enough?" he asked me.

"I don't know. When did she say she'd be back?"

The biggest problem, of course, was food rather than sex. Well, at least the biggest immediate problem. Chuck and I solved this by eating watermelons and drinking Fanta. We would take turns going up to the counter in the bazaar through the cloud of wasps that also seemed able to survive on watermelons and Fanta. We would negotiate the price of a watermelon, get four bottles of Fanta, and ignore the dozens of yellow jackets buzzing around our faces, landing on our hands and in our hair.

It could take up to five minutes to buy a watermelon, and you couldn't appear to be in a hurry or bothered by what was going on around you. First, you and the shopkeeper had to agree on a price per pound. Going to the same shopkeeper two or three times a day didn't speed this up: every transaction was a brand-new event, which must start at square one. Then, once you decided the price for yak pow of watermelon, you had to decide how many pows it was. The shopkeeper would put the watermelon on one side of a scale and then put various heavy things on the other side of the scale; scrap metal, for the most part, with transmission gears being one of the favorites. At first, we thought this was standardized—that first gear in a Bedford truck equaled one pound, something along these lines—but, while the act of selecting a piece of metal was an extraordinary dramatization of painfully careful deliberation, the actual selection was utterly random. Or more accurately, utterly self-interested within the bounds of plausibility. So we would stand there, waving our arms at the shopkeeper without waving them fast enough to frighten or anger the wasps: "*Yak pow n'ais*," we'd say, "That isn't a pound. That one over there. Use that gear." It was scary doing this, sweating and covered with wasps, but it wasn't as frightening as going into any of the local restaurants.

We knew this was a temporary solution. We knew we couldn't really live on sugar water. We also knew that we had been in Afghanistan long enough to lose whatever excess weight we carried. On the positive side, living on watermelons and Fanta meant that we probably wouldn't get sick and we could avoid bowel movements.

Avoiding bowel movements was important. We were men, after all, so peeing presented no real problems. But there was an outhouse in the far rear corner of our yard and that was where bowel movements were supposed to take place. It was as foul a place as can be imagined. From the outside, it looked like a standard-issue outhouse, not much different from the ones which could be found in rural America not so long ago and which have now been transformed into the Porta-Potties we see at road construction sites and in the fields at harvest time. Chuck drew a picture of a half-moon and put it on the door. Inside, however, there was simply a hole in the ground about a foot across, which had been used with varying degrees of accuracy for a long time by people with serious intestinal problems. There was a small window high on one wall that let in the little light that dared to enter. The trick, as mentioned earlier in the description of the Tehran airport, was to ensure that absolutely nothing we valued touched anything at all . . . and to do this while holding one's breath. We had both used it once already, having foolishly eaten solid food on our last day in Kabul, and now it stood there: a fly-covered, stench-filled monument to the biological processes involved in converting matter to energy. Chuck's experience had been worse than mine, because at a crucial moment in the balancing process a camel had stuck its head in the tiny window to see what he was doing.

I think we went three days on the watermelon-Fanta diet before we finally admitted to ourselves that we simply had to get something more substantial to eat. We walked to the town square and went into one of the tea shops.

Like all the shops in Laghman, this one was about ten or twelve feet across, seven feet high, and very deep. There was a row of tables down the right wall. On the left, as you entered, was the samovar used to boil the water for tea and a large cast-iron pot filled with stew. There was no menu, but there were a number of choices. We could have tea, tea and food, or food alone. We opted for tea and food.

This was the last time my nose worked until I left Afghanistan. At some point, just after sitting down, I realized that there is a switch deep in the brain that simply allows the olfactory sense to be turned off. I switched it off immediately as a hindrance to survival: if I had to smell it, I wouldn't eat it and if I didn't eat it, I would die. Air, and God knows what else, was free to waft in and out of my nose, but all connections to my brain were put on hold until further notice. At least until winter.

We were probably the first Westerners ever to sit down in this restaurant. Chuck was handicapped with bright blue eyes and there were times when it seemed he literally couldn't get his teacup to his lips because someone was in the way, staring at his eyes. The owner pulled a rag out of his pocket and wiped off the bowls before ladling in the stew. He put the bowls on the table and asked if everything was good. We assured him it was, and then we looked at the food.

I grew to love this stew. It is served all over the country, in varying forms. There is a basic reddish-brown sauce with vegetables, potatoes, and animal parts. I eat oxtail stew in Chinese-American restaurants and am reminded of the Afghan stew. But the first time one encounters this dish, it requires an act of will to consume it. I ate the potatoes first because they were recognizable, even though they were probably turnips. But there were not more than three or four pieces of potato-turnips in my bowl and then I had to move on. We had been given bread—the flat, Afghan "snowshoe" bread—and we used that, dipping it into the stew. I ate all the pieces of meat that looked like pieces of meat, ignoring everything that required interpretation. I waved my left hand slowly over the bowl to keep the flies from landing. If they wanted stew, let them eat it out of the pot like all their friends. We drank the tea.

I think we finished about half the food. Our goal had not been actually to eat, as to prove to ourselves that we could do it without either going into convulsions or throwing up and embarrassing ourselves and our hosts.

When the owner cleared our table, Chuck said, "He's going to dump this back into the pot." And, of course, the owner did, using one of our spoons to make sure that all the sauce and various pieces of things were not wasted. We watched him wipe the bowls clean with his rag. Nothing is wasted in Afghanistan.

"Well," I said, after a moment, "we just can't think about it."

Chuck nodded. "Not if we want to live."

WATERMELONS, PART TWO

I REMEMBER THE MINUTE WHEN I FIRST CONSIDERED GOING INTO the Peace Corps. I had been sitting in a philosophy seminar with three other students. The class was so unpopular that we could all fit in the professor's office, so that's where we had class. The professor was playing philosophy games. Philosophy games take place when really articulate adults defend to the death the ideas of precocious eight-year-olds: Maybe I am not here. I can't really feel the desk because feeling is a sensation and sensations are in my brain. You don't know where you live. Maybe what's blue to you is red to me, but we have no way of knowing. As I left his office after a particularly stupefying three hours, it occurred to me that I desperately needed something a little more concrete than a commitment to clever ignorance. Just as I turned to go down the stairs, I remembered seeing the Peace Corps poster outside one of the more obscure offices on campus.

I mention this because one of the philosophical puzzles that always bothered me was the idea that the little weights used by the people from the Office of Weights and Measures didn't weigh anything. Imagine, if you can, a small guarded office in Washington in which there is a locked drawer. In the locked drawer there are small weights and rulers. All rulers are judged for accuracy against the ruler in the drawer. All weights are judged for accuracy against the weights in the drawer. You could take their one-pound weight into your local market, put it on one of their produce scales and see if the scales are accurate. It would make no sense, it was argued, to say that the block of steel weighed a pound. It was a pound. It was, in some sense, the meaning of pound.

This bothered me on and off during my student years. It was like a loose tooth or the lyrics from a particularly annoying pop song.

It was in Laghman that I came to appreciate this idea. On a scale, there can only be one thing that has weight: the bag of rice, the piece of meat, your body. On the other side of the scale are the weighing criteria, which have no weight in the context in which they are used. Or, as I learned to talk when I became a researcher, when weighing something, there can only be one variable. You cannot ask both "What does the piece of meat weigh?" and "What do the weights weigh?" at the same time. (I suppose you could say that John Doe weighs 170 pounds and that this bunch of weights together weigh one John Doe, but I am not sure why one would want to do that.)

Laghman gave me my first real understanding of this sort of thinking. In Laghman, both the weight of the object to be purchased and the weight of the object used as the criteria for weighing were in question. Everything was negotiable. There was no way to find out what the second gear of a Bedford truck weighed, so it didn't really weigh anything in any sense we would recognize. There was nothing in this system which was a given, and it took a while to get used to having to argue for both the value and the nature of something at the same time. And, of course, the two things were related in that the less I wanted to pay per "pound," the more "pounds" I would have to pay for. I tried to circumvent this conundrum by bargaining directly for the watermelon (I'll give you ten afghani for the watermelon), but the shopkeepers wouldn't play this game. They insisted on selling watermelons by the pound.

This said an awful lot about Afghan society. First, it said that efficiency was not a core value. I could do a week's shopping in Safeway without speaking to anyone, in the time it would take to buy a few cigarettes, a couple of eggs, and some salt in Kabul. Second, since every interaction was a complex, subtle negotiation, it said that the social elements of life were extremely important.

Bartering was an enjoyable process in which people developed strategies, read non-verbal cues, and learned to tell stories. It was never adversarial. It was always an effort to come to some agreement about what was best for both the people involved and that, of course, meant we had to accept that it might be best if one person paid slightly more for something than someone else paid. The closest thing to this in the United States, I think, would be buying a used car from a private party.

Finally, life from this perspective is a fluid thing. American life is amazingly rigid. We have reduced the levels of uncertainty so that we don't have to spend time thinking about mundane things. When you buy a watermelon in Afghanistan, you have to be engaged, your brain has to be in gear. This is very different from going into McDonald's and asking for a Number Two Value Meal. Or going to the supermarket and having the clerk scan your watermelon, where it's quite possible that neither you nor the grocery clerk are conscious of how much you actually paid. Daily life in America becomes a background in which more specific actions take place. The background becomes like white noise, and so what counts as sound is much more narrowly defined.

Social interaction with strangers fades into the background in the U.S. and we redefine social life as private life, or personal life. And, of course, once social life is defined in personal terms, social life in the sense of public life dwindles to almost nothing. And so we develop a society in which interaction is unnecessary: cash machines, self-service gas stations, drive-up windows, pay-for-view, on-line shopping, telecommuting, fixed prices, scanning cash registers. It's a long list.

This radically shrinks everyone's experience with society because there is less and less need to speak with strangers. And, speaking with strangers has become increasingly formulaic: Do you want to supersize that? Have a nice day. Can I get anything else for you guys? Even the beggars hold up their signs, advertising their condition rather than discussing it.

An additional cultural problem for me was that Afghans separated the idea of fairness from the idea of universality. Basically, if you jump out of your Mercedes, you are going to pay more for a watermelon than if you get off a bus. And if you really don't want to buy a watermelon as much as someone wants to sell you one, then you will pay less than if this were reversed. If each exchange is relatively self-contained, and the goal in each exchange is for the individuals to reach a satisfactory conclusion, then the conclusions could vary substantially.

In the West, however, there has been a huge effort to standardize things—mechanical parts, hamburgers, and outcomes—so the idea that I would pay more for the same thing than someone else would is almost self-evidently unfair. While I may concede that I can or should pay more than an Afghan would (because I am comparatively well off), it would really strike me as unfair if I had to pay more than Chuck. I had to get used to this. My outcome had nothing to do with Chuck's outcome.

The negotiating culture is also based very strongly in mutual regard. In individualistic America, the best deal is not one in which both parties are satisfied. The best deal is when I get what I want, and I don't care what you get. MP3 and Napster are evidence of this: the best price you can pay for music is nothing. And the rationale for this is "You can't stop me." (It is usually put differently, of course. It is more like It's inevitable or Everyone is doing it or It's the way things are now or, most simply, What's the problem?) Corporations are major proponents of this perspective, as well, in their endless search for cheaper and more desperate labor: ideally, people would work for them for nothing. That would be the best deal.

Increasingly, I think we Americans have confused being individualistic with being anti-social. That would account for our being so standoffish and yet such major fans of standardization.

CAMPING

LIVING IN THE RURAL AREAS OF AFGHANISTAN IS LIKE CAMPING. The house we had in Laghman was one room. The floor was packed dirt with a woven mat to keep the dust down. Afghans used something that looked to me like palm fronds to create floor coverings over which you would lay rugs. If you wanted to install a new floor covering, a crew would come in and all the men would squat down at one end of the room and start braiding or weaving the leaves together. When the floors coverings were new, they were bright green and cool to the touch, but they quickly yellowed and formed a very durable surface. You had to have rugs down, though, because Afghans, like most civilized people, did not wear their shoes inside their houses, and palm splinters in the soles of your feet were nothing to laugh at.

When the Afghans put down the new floor in Chuck's house in Kabul (this was much later), there was only an occasional, softly-worded exchange. Otherwise they just worked, lost in thought, and caught up in the rhythm of it. I always liked watching Afghans work because Afghanistan was a country with very little sound. Afghans seemed aware of that and so, with the exception of music blaring from loudspeakers on all the long-haul trucks, the place was almost silent.

The reason people didn't wear shoes inside was because there was so much shit outside. Shit, literally. In this sense, Afghan walkways were even worse than sidewalks in France, although in Afghanistan it was human rather than canine poop. Because there was so much crap every where, you had to assume that some of it got on your shoes. It didn't matter how careful you were. This wasn't even taking into consideration all the pissing and spitting. Like everywhere else it's practiced, taking off your shoes when entering had become a symbolic gesture indicating respect for someone else's home.

When we set up house in Laghman, we used the rickety blue table we found outside as our one piece of furniture. We put our wash basin on top of that and hung a little shaving mirror on the wall. We had a woven rug of no value that we spread over the worn palm leaves. On top of that, we put down our sleeping mats that were about sleeping-bag size and filled with cotton batting. If you put one on top of another, you got a fairly comfortable mattress.

The number of rats that ran over us the first night were really alarming. They lived in the walls and under the palm leaves and you could hear them all night long, rustling around and fighting. We just made sure we were completely covered by our blankets, which was difficult given the heat, and let them run wherever they wanted. It wasn't as if we had a choice. It became increasingly difficult to scare them away. One night I woke up when two of them decided to play on top of me and it wasn't until I stood up that they reluctantly ran off.

The rats were only a problem for the first few weeks and then they either left the house or simply became bored with trying to freak us out every night. Or we learned to ignore them.

There was also a problem with the wasps that lived in the walls. Near the door, there was a small hole that was the entrance to their nest. Chuck and I would watch them flying in and out of it when we sat in our little patch of shade on the two chairs that we had found. We would sit in the chairs in the afternoon, after getting off work. Mostly we read books from the Peace Corps library, but sometimes we'd talk and sometimes we'd just sit, staring at the fence across the yard. I really hated the wasps. Chuck was more cautiously tolerant. One day, I couldn't stand them anymore, so I put down my slice of watermelon and went into the house and got the can of insect repellent that Kay had left for us.

"I think that is going to be a mistake," Chuck said, as he watched me planning my attack on the wasps' nest. There were two or three wasps trying to get to his watermelon. He waved them gently aside.

It wasn't much of a hole, but then wasps don't require much. It was a wide part of a crack in the cement near the doorframe, not much more than a half-inch across. Traffic was pretty steady, with one or two always on their way in and an equal number on their way out. They were nasty-looking things, with their tiny waists and black and yellow coloring.

"I think this is really going to piss them off," Chuck said.

"They'll be pissed off, but then they'll be trapped in the wall. This is the only entrance they're using, so I can just seal them in." I had a plan.

"I don't think it's going to work." He was just expressing an opinion rather than offering any sort of suggestion.

I thought about that for a minute. It seemed to me that we had to do something. We were Americans, after all, and we had to act aggressively in first defining things as problems and then in solving them, through violence if possible. "Well, here goes," I told him. I stepped forward, pushed the nozzle against the crack and emptied about half the can into the wall. I then ran back and stood next to Chuck. We were about ten feet away. We sipped our Fantas and watched. I was standing. Chuck was still sitting down.

A few wasps, on their way into the wall, backed off, hovering. Yes, I thought, go live somewhere else. One wasp came out of the crack, staggered to the edge of the hole and fell dramatically to the ground. It was very Shakespearean. Another simply bumbled his way out and fell on top of his more accomplished predecessor. Then nothing happened.

"See?" I said. "They're all stuck in there and can't get out."

"We'll see," Chuck told me. He was, by nature, a skeptic.

And then the stream began. It was as if the house had turned into some sort of wasp gun, shooting out a steady stream of wasps. It looked like hundreds of them, thousands of them. Fortunately for us, they streamed straight out over the roof.

Chuck jumped out of his chair when he saw them. "Sealed them in, all right," he said.

It was like a black and yellow cord connecting the sky to our doorway. "Let's go into town."

"Good idea."

We ran out of the yard, laughing like maniacs.

The wasps were back the next day and we just learned to live with them.

We also learned to accept brushing our teeth without using water. We learned to shave in lukewarm water, heated in our teapot with our electric coil, then dumped into a washbasin. Afghans shaved only every three or four days, from the looks of them. This was in the pre-Taliban days when only religious leaders were bearded. We never adopted this practice of shaving twice a week, not even when we were reduced to using Chinese Happiness Razor Blades, which were not designed for men with actual beards. Later, when I was in the North, I would drag that damned Happiness Blade over my face every morning and end up looking like a clean-shaven victim of some bizarre accident.

Kay would drive down to visit us, to make sure we were surviving. Once, when she was leaving, she asked if we needed anything. "More condoms," Chuck said, standing in the dead red dust of our yard. "We're all out."

She came down one day when we were in the middle of washing our clothes. They were soaking in soapy water in a large galvanized tub. Against her better judgement, we talked her into taking us back to Kabul for the weekend. We were thinking Bright Lights, Big City. Or, at least, we were thinking we could get a chance to talk to some women before we forgot how to do it. (Chuck told everyone that he and I had a bet on who would have the first wet dream and that he won the first night.)

"What about your clothes?" she asked. And we pulled them out of the water, frenzied, as if we wanted this objection to go away as fast as possible. We threw the sodden mess into our laundry bags, and took them to Kay's house to be dried in her dryer. Kay's husband was at the U.S. Embassy so they had a washer and dryer.

It never occurred to us that we wouldn't find a place to stay. Peace Corps volunteers can show up unannounced at any other volunteer's house and be invited to stay. "Invited to stay," is actually too formal. A Peace Corps volunteer can stay at any other volunteer's house for a few days without anyone thinking anything about it. You just hang around the office until someone comes in and tell him, "I'm in for a day or so," and her takes you to his house.

Chuck and I threw our wet bags of laundry into the Land Cruiser and jumped in before Kay could make any further objections. Chuck was in the front seat and I was in the back, sitting in the middle, leaning forward. It was on this trip that the miracle occurred.

The Kabul Gorge is a giant crack in the side of the plateau on which the capital sits. The road climbs (or drops, of course, depending on your direction) through a series of harrowing switchbacks. It's a narrow, two lane road, with the cliff face on one side and a sheer drop on the other. For the most part, there is no shoulder: there's the road, about two feet of crumbling soil, and a drop of a few hundred feet to the river below.

Much later, when I was living in the North, Ed and Chuck rode bicycles down the road. It was a feat of daring that I always envied. You couldn't have more than minimal control because the road is so steep that the bicycle brakes would be basically worthless. The brakes would simply provide something to do with your hands while you ran headlong into the cliff, off the edge, or under the truck lumbering its way toward you.

We were in the Toyota Land Cruiser and all the other vehicles on the road were either Bedford trucks or dilapidated buses. The Bedford trucks looked to me to be about two-and-a-half-ton trucks. They looked, that is, about the size of the trucks used by the U.S. Army to haul around its soldiers. These trucks, as mentioned earlier, were garishly decorated with painted script, tasseled cabs, loudspeakers blaring Afghan and Persian music, mirrors, and everything colorful which could conceivably make its way into Afghanistan and be attached somehow to a moving vehicle. Mechanically, they were noisy, smoking pieces of junk with loose steering, bad brakes and crappy suspensions.

We rounded one curve to see two of these trucks filling the entire road. It was a short straight section of the road and one of the trucks was trying to pass the other, both of them heading in our direction. The angle of the road made their speeds about equal, the passing truck barely inching its way past its very slightly slower brother. He was on our side of the road and we had nowhere to go.

"Oh, shit," someone said, and then no one said anything else. There was nothing else to say. Kay slowed way down and moved over as far as she could. We could feel the outside wheels digging into the dirt ledge between the paved surface and the cliff edge. Getting over as far as she did was a gesture. She did it because you have to do something, but it was about as useful as standing on only one of the tracks on the train trestle as the train barreled toward you. She was braking as hard as she could, trying to give the Bedford room to get back to its side of the road. The Bedford made no effort to slow at all and instead remained committed to its attempt to pass the slower truck: it was, I think, the driver's only option.

And then we ran out of room. Kay said something, I think, as the oncoming truck filled our windshield. Good bye or oh, well; something along those lines. At the moment of impact, I closed my eyes.

But the impact didn't come. I opened my eyes just as Kay swerved back onto the road. "What happened?" I asked.

"I don't know," she said.

"Neither do I," Chuck said.

We had all blinked, and in the duration of the blink, the truck had disappeared. We all turned and saw it rocketing down the road, on the proper side, swaying on its derelict suspension, and we had no idea how it happened. We had all blinked at the last possible moment, when there was absolutely no way that we weren't going to get in a head-on collision and get punted out into the gorge.

Except that we didn't.

GOING TO WORK

THE SCHOOL PRINCIPAL STOOD OUTSIDE WHERE THE LAWN would have been had there been a lawn. He spoke with the students as they straggled into school, looking very much like students everywhere; some noisy, some apprehensive, some unable to move without dropping a book or a pencil. It was eight in the morning, but the heat was already settling in for the day, pressing the ground flat and robbing the sky of any color. The principal said hello to many of the students and it appeared that he knew them all. Part of his job every morning was to hurry along the students who were in danger of being late. In school, although nowhere else in Afghan society, punctuality was considered extremely important.

The future is in the hands of God, we were told, so it was a bit presumptuous to make plans or have deadlines. This is the explanation for the famous lack of time-consciousness that is found in Islamic societies. Or, at least, it was the explanation we were given. Another more prosaic explanation is that almost no one had a watch and there was a real shortage of clocks. So every morning I would watch the children being punished for being late and would try to imagine them at home, riddled with anxiety, trying to figure out when to leave for school. "The sun is up and the rooster crowed," one would say. "But Abdul has not yet walked past," his brother might object, "and he always walks past before we leave." "Adbul is sick." "Oh, crap." "I think the shadows are longer."

There's a cause-and-effect problem with these two explanations: religion versus a shortage of clocks. Or a chicken-and-egg problem. Why don't they have clocks? Why do they think the future is in the hands of God? In the West, clocks became important when train schedules had to be maintained and industrial activities coordinated. Prior to that, clocks were toys used by the monks to organize their prayers. It was difficult to imagine a peasant putting down his cup of morning coffee and saying, "Eight-fifteen. Time to feed the chickens."

We learned that westerners called Ariana Airlines, the country's airline, Inshallah Airlines. Inshallah meant something like "God willing." Whenever you planned to meet someone, you always would say God willing. Of course, each night, my father who was a Catholic, would say that he would see us the next morning "with the help of God." For years, my brothers and I said "hepagod" when anyone said good night to us. "Goodnight." "Hepagod." Inshallah.

Functionally, inshallah meant something like "if we're lucky" or "I guess so." Every new Westerner was told endless stories about showing up five minutes early to an 11:00 appointment that ended up taking place at 1:15. This was attributed to either the Islamic aversion to time or to different social norms. I thought that power differences and differences in social status accounted for a lot of it. Subordinates did not keep superiors waiting.

Afghans always wanted to know what time it was. "*Chand ba'jas?*" they would ask if we walked past them on the road as they ambled along patiently, pulling a donkey or using a stick to guide some reluctant sheep. We would always make a big production of looking at our watches. "It's two-forty-three," we'd tell them, if that were the time, and they would nod their heads in satisfaction, obviously right on schedule. Sometimes, I wanted to ask them what difference knowing the time could possibly make, but I never did. I think they simply like knowing about time, or knowing that people like me had a name for every possible moment and that they could never catch us unprepared. "You want to know what time is it now? Hmm, it appears there is no time right now, but if you wait a while then, inshallah, there will be time again. Perhaps tomorrow."

I must admit that it felt strange wearing a watch in Afghanistan. It may be that in the land of the blind, the man with one eye is king. But, in a land without time, a man with a watch seems like something of an idiot.

Chuck had been a teacher in Pennsylvania. Chuck had been many things; a teacher, an Army Ranger, a man who could build a house with his own two hands, a wickedly ambidextrous Ping-Pong player, and a man who ruined his hands and his dreams in a brief moment of generosity when he changed a woman's tire just because he was feeling so good that he had to help, had no choice but to help. The hubcap had sliced through all the tendons in the fingers of one hand and changed the course of his life. His was a life changed by silly things, it seemed; the hubcap, a booby-trapped trashcan that exploded, bursting his eardrums and keeping him out of Vietnam. He was a man of tremendous exuberance and it cracked me up on our first day of class that he was told to report to a table outside the school building.

"Is the table the classroom?" he whispered to me as we were led across the schoolyard. He was carrying his chalkboard. We had both been given chalkboards. In Afghanistan, I discovered there is something called blackboard paint. You paint a piece of wood and it becomes something like a blackboard. Blackboards are expensive: you carry one around and don't let it out of your sight.

"I don't know. I think so." There were twenty-five or thirty children gathered around the table.

"Jeez," he said. "Where are you going?"

"Into the building, I guess." A student aide was leading me. "Golly, Chuck, I guess they just figured you didn't need a classroom." I think he wanted to flip me off, but there were hundreds of people watching us, so he just gave me a dismissive wave and went over to his picnic table.

I was led into the building and that's when I realized it was just a shell. They build of brick in Afghanistan and so all the walls were up, but the floors in the entry and central hall were just rough uneven concrete to be finished at some later date. Off the hallway, the classrooms had swept dirt floors. There were no windows, no doors, no roof. There were holes where the doors and windows would eventually go. There was no indication that this would be happening anytime soon.

The students sat on benches without desks. There was a chair in the front on which I could prop the blackboard. They were, I think, fourth graders. I was there to teach them English and they sat fairly quietly, watching the strange foreigner trying to get acclimated.

There was a law in Afghanistan that everyone had to learn a foreign language. English was the most common, because of the Peace Corps, but they also learned French, German, and Russian. It just depended on where they went to school. There was also a law that when going to school, the students had to wear Western coats. So, over their traditional clothing, each of the boys wore a sport coat. The coats arrived in huge bales from charities in West Germany.

It was a little slow getting started because it took a while to figure out what they knew. I would spend the first week going over the earlier lessons. This group was at the See Spot run level. Teaching English as a Second Language is tremendous fun because it is a combination of phonetics and rote memory, which means that you drill on the lesson for the entire class. It becomes game-like and interactive. I worked with them for forty minutes and then the assistant principal walked by the empty window-hole ringing a bell. Class was over.

My next class was under the tree near the gate.

CHICKEN BUS TO JALALABAD

THE NEAREST CITY WAS JALALABAD. JALALABAD WAS ON THE road to the Khyber Pass and, past that, to Pakistan. These days, it is probably best known as the road through one of Al Qaeda's last strongholds. When I was there, the Khyber Pass was famous because the British lost their final battle there when they were driven from Afghanistan.

Afghanistan is full of passes and gorges. Chuck and I used to plan military campaigns to take over the country and they always ended up focusing on three places: the Khyber Pass (to prevent or allow resupply, depending on our scenario), the Kabul Gorge, and the Salang Pass. The only ways to get to Kabul on land involved going up the Kabul Gorge (from the south) or over the Salang Pass (from the north). Ignoring air power, you'd need only a few well-placed groups of people to shut down transport to the capital. It could probably be done with a few hundred people, operating in small weapons teams.

This is one of the things Chuck and I used to talk about as we lay on the thick stone fence that bounded our property in Laghman. Typical Peace Corps conversation: how to take over the nation in which you are volunteering. We'd lie on the warm stone, the backs of our heads almost touching so that we could talk, somewhere up-wind of the outhouse, and stare at the night sky. The air was so clear that the sky appeared three-dimensional and the depth of space could be seen. Once, we saw a satellite arcing

its way across the sky, almost in line with our fence. It was heading north, we thought, most likely in order to spy on the Soviet
Union. It was odd seeing it, like a little bit of home: something we
had made, like the paper bags at the grocery store.

Afghanistan is not Italy. If you went to live in Italy or France
for two years, there would be a huge class of people pretty much
like yourself—middle-class business people, academics, artists
. . . whatever you happened to be. You would meet them at work
and eventually be invited out for a drink or over for dinner. You
could sit in cafes and strike up conversations, or go to nightclubs
and engage in trans-cultural activities like drinking, dancing, and
flirting. But there were no opportunities to go drinking, dancing,
or flirting with Afghans.

This makes it very difficult to get to know Afghans. Or at
least, it makes it very difficult to get to know them quickly. The
traditional Western avenues for making connections or becoming
friends simply did not exist. In order to get deeper into Afghan
culture, I had to learn to become less of an American, less of
a Westerner. But the country was so radically different that it
seemed our Americanness was reinforced, bolstered, ballooned
out of proportion, until it became our primary identity. Sort of
like Chuck's blue eyes.

This was somewhat ironic, because Peace Corps volunteers
tended to see themselves as internationalists, their American identity somewhat blurred by the adoption of a more global perspective. And, again, in a more familiar environment we could have
concealed our identities to a greater extent and thus become more
integrated into the local society. But in Afghanistan, and especially in Laghman, there were so many barriers: our unfamiliarity
with the culture and country, our status as teachers, our appear-
ance, various laws, political divisions, and the fact that we were
living in a very provincial region.

Laghman was not a large town. When I had come through
with Jessie, Ed, and Melissa, we had seen the whole town twice.
And then Jessie and I stayed over while Ed and Melissa went on to
Jalalabad and we had walked all over the countryside. Jessie had

legs about two miles long and walked at a rapid pace, so there was very little we hadn't seen. Eventually, Chuck and I looked at every shop in town, talked with every shop owner. Everyone knew we were the new *ma'lem-sahibs* at the school. Chuck and I also had the dubious benefit of a self-imposed guide called Fukir Jon. He reminded me of the person who takes you under his or her wing when you are new at a job, and who, inevitably, is the last person you should ever listen to. Fucker John, as we came to call him, showed us around town. We noticed that Fucker John had a questionable status among the locals and that we got some odd looks when we showed up with him in tow. There were political undercurrents that we could feel, but did not understand.

———

Jalalabad, just down the road heading toward Pakistan, had some actual restaurants in addition to tea shops serving stew. Chuck and I went there a few times to get something to eat. Jalalabad was more fun to wander around than Laghman, simply because it was big enough that I didn't have it memorized after one or two walks down all the streets. I liked going there more than Chuck did, so twice I went alone. The last time I went, the trip out and the time spent in Jalalabad were uneventful, but coming back was interesting.

The first problem was that all the bus drivers assumed that I wanted to go either west to Kabul, south to Kandahar, or east to Pakistan, because there was no reason for a foreigner to go to Laghman. Once I determined which bus went back to Laghman, I got on and sat in the seat right behind the driver.

Foreigners are supposed to sit in the first two rows. This is also where the women are supposed to sit, so sometimes this involves a little jockeying because I was not allowed to sit next to a woman.

There were buses all around us, rattling and pumping out clouds of greasy black diesel smoke, which floated lazily around the buses in the windless afternoon. People went to Jalalabad to go to the bazaar, so after a while the bazaar blended into the bus stop to form one wonderfully chaotic, colorful swirl of activity. I sat sideways on the seat directly behind the driver, sipping a Fanta and smoking a cigarette, watching people carrying chickens and roosters onto the bus. The bus was full of diesel fumes from the truck next to us and, to further increase the richness of the experience, the smell of spoiled vegetables or human shit would occasionally waft in and assault us. Sometimes a chicken would panic, or bump into another chicken, and then there would be sudden squawks and flapping of wings while the men tried to soothe them back into a stupor. Men wrestled ungainly packages, wrapped in newsprint or cloth and tied with string, into the overhead racks or onto the roof with the quiet seriousness with which they tend to work.

I watched the women as much as I could, using the driver's mirror and the reflections in the windows. There were two in the row behind me, on the other side of the bus. They spoke together in whispers, their heads touching, and the cloth of their chadors flattening the tips of their noses and flowing softly over the curves of their breasts. They were like the chickens, I thought, that were calm when held upside down. These women were calm, caught and held in bags in the stifling heat. Or, perhaps that was just my projections, but I knew of no society in which men constrained themselves to this extent and, being a little claustrophobic, I thought that if I had to wear all-enveloping clothing that I would force myself to live in a continuous zen state, burying panic and frustration so deep that it became something else.

I had finished my Fanta, so I went out to give the bottle back to the shopkeeper, walking carefully in the yellow dirt, smeared with dark stains from Godknowswhat, with flies buzzing heavily in the sun and the low voices of the men standing—barely visible—in the deep shade of the shops. The smells were sharp in my nose and the light dazzling as it played over the flat surfaces. This was a country to love, I thought. It confronted you without ambiguity. It was always there, overwhelming you with the sheer, unrelenting reality of it all; a place that could not be ignored and to which it was impossible to grow accustomed.

When I reboarded the bus, a man was standing near my seat. He was wearing a sport coat, so he wasn't a farmer in town to buy chickens. He was a man with an official or semi-official role in society, a man who thought well of himself. We said hello to each other, asked how we were doing.

"Are you sitting here?" he asked me in Farsi, pointing at my seat. I had left a book on my seat and apparently that had caught his attention.

I told him I was, and he seemed not to like it. It was interesting, this seat thing. I didn't like being told to sit with the women. I especially didn't like being told this by men who didn't, by the standards that shaped me, seem to have a very high opinion of women. It bothered me that I was insulted by this, but within this culture being lumped in with the women was an insult. On the other hand, I wasn't really being told to sit with the women—actually, I was not allowed to share a seat with an Afghan woman—I was told to sit in the front. Being told to sit in the front is like being given the first seat or the seat at the head of the table. Looked at this way, it is an honor to be asked to sit in the front of the bus. It is in this second sense that the man in the sport coat interpreted my location.

"Why are you going to Laghman? There is nothing there for you."

"I live in Laghman. I am a teacher there."

He turned to the rest of the people on the bus. He said, quite loudly, "Excuse me, my friends, this man is sitting in the front because he says he is a teacher." Everyone was now looking at us. "I am a teacher and I do not know him."

This was interesting. "I am a teacher," I told the other passengers. "I am new in Laghman. This man and I have never met."

He turned to me. "What do you teach?" I told him I was an English teacher. "He claims," he told our audience in Farsi, "to be an English teacher, yet I am an English teacher and do not know him."

He then turned to me and said something which, to the best of my memory, sounded like, "Hmmm baggle derump minueto."

I assumed we were still speaking in Farsi, so I told him I didn't understand. He scowled in contempt. "He claims to be an English teacher," he announced to the rest of the bus, "yet when I speak to him in English, he doesn't understand." The passengers were now interested. Who was this imposter? they wondered. I asked him to repeat his remark.

"Hmmm baggle derump minueto."

"I'm sorry," I said in English. "I don't understand what you are saying."

"Then you are not an English teacher," he said in Farsi.

I showed him my book, which was written in English. He told me that anyone could buy a book, that meant nothing. "Do you know," he asked me, "the five verbs?"

"In English?"

"Yes. Do you know the five verbs in English?"

I shook my head. "I don't know what you mean. Do you mean five verb tenses? Do you mean five conjugations?"

He laughed contemptuously and turned to the other passengers. "He says he is an English teacher, yet he doesn't know the five verbs."

I was really confused. "What are the five verbs?"

"He asked me what are the five verbs. Everyone knows that the five verbs are minnoo, pinti, dragle, goshen, lickensplat." (I just made those up, but they aren't far off.)

"Do you know what this means?" I asked him. "Your grandmother eats shit." I said it slowly.

"That is not English."

"Here," I said. "Let me write it down. If you have a good dictionary in English, you will figure it out." I wrote the sentence on a piece of paper and gave it to him. He looked at it very carefully, then folded it and put it in his pocket. I sat down and a minute or two later the driver boarded and we were on our way.

As near as I could figure, this man had been taught English by someone who had been taught English by a native speaker of English. In the interim, he had probably rarely or never actually heard anyone speak the language. In some small village in Laghman Province, he taught a version of English grammar based in someone else's memory of what it sounded like. I wondered if his dictionary had shit in it and, if not, how long he carried around that piece of paper until he found out what it meant.

When I got back to Laghman, I found Chuck in the house, lying on his mat, propped on an elbow, reading. "Hey," I said. "Let me ask you something."

"Okay." He marked his place in his book with a finger.

"Can you tell me what the five verbs are in English?"

"What?"

"Good. That's all I wanted to know."

"What are you talking about? What verbs?"

So I told him the story of the chicken bus.

DINNER IN LAGHMAN

"Sure," we said. "We would like that very much."

He was another teacher in the school and had just invited us over for dinner. This was an amazing thing. It was a breakthrough. And not only in the sense that we were being presented with an opportunity to supplement our diet of watermelons, Fantas, and Chai Hanna stew; it was a social breakthrough, our first step into Laghman society. Up until now, we had walked the surface, not so much knocking on doors as exchanging glances through windows, and now someone was going to let us inside.

A boy, we were told, would come for us and take us to the house. It must have been on a Friday, which is a half-day of work in Afghanistan, because I remember working that day, before hurrying home through the dusty streets. The boy was going to meet us at our house but of course the time element was vague so we wanted to make sure we were there when he arrived.

Chuck and I didn't get dressed up. We didn't jump into the shower or do any of the things one might do under similar circumstances in the U.S. We had no clothes more decent than the ones we were wearing and we didn't have a shower. So we went home, brewed some tea and sat around reading, until the boy showed up late in the afternoon.

He took us out of town. We followed him down dirt trails, along rice levees, and across fields to a compound of considerable size. Afghans build homes that look like forts. There are high, thick walls around the perimeter of the property. The house and the barn are inside and use the perimeter wall as one of the walls of the structures. This, I think, is a fairly traditional way of building. Italian country houses were built this way, and what are now beautiful courtyards in Tuscany were originally barnyards.

We entered through double wooden gates and then were shown into the house. Chuck and I had some academic knowledge of what to expect. We knew the basic rules of etiquette—eat whatever is served, don't refuse seconds, don't take food with your left hand, take off your shoes—but beyond that, we didn't really have a clue.

We were welcomed and went to sit in a long, narrow room, on a red Afghan "elephant footprint" rug. It was an enormous rug that would have cost a fortune in the United States. Here, it was nice, but it was also just a rug, so we could eat on it without worrying about dropping the odd grain of rice on the floor. The teacher, his father, and his son joined us around the carpet while the women hovered in the next room. They would eat after we were finished. They would probably eat whatever we left. On the way here, Chuck and I had talked about two problems. The first problem was that, because of our recent fear-of-food, we had stomachs the size of chickpeas. This would make the obligatory second serving a little difficult. One thing that never occurred to us was that the food would be inedible or unhealthy: we were looking forward to this meal. The second problem was a moral one, wrapped in ignorance: how much food can we eat without looking like inconsiderate gluttons? This was a matter of cultural niceties, requiring finesse and a deft hand, neither of which we had.

We drank tea and chatted. The teacher spoke English better than we spoke Farsi, but neither side was really fluent. We developed a hybrid language, using words we knew from both languages, as needed. Chuck was pretty good at this sort of improvising. He had developed a way of speaking Farsi without using a lot of verbs, and he did it so well that, while you knew at some level something was missing, it was never bothersome. We realized almost immediately that this was going to be a very civilized meal, sitting on the floor of this farmhouse, preparing to eat with our hands. The pace was slow and relaxed. We were here to spend the evening: no McKabobs here, no gobble and run. After a long while, the meal was served: heaping mounds of saffron rice and a complete chicken for each of us. Chuck and I exchanged glances. This was not going to be easy. I felt bloated just looking at my plate.

We set to work, Chuck and I. I learned that the technique described in training for eating rice with one's hands was nowhere near as neat as I had been led to believe. Eating chicken without utensils results in greasy hands. This is common knowledge. But when it's combined with eating rice, you end up with rice grains all over your hands and no way to wipe them off. The meal, though, was absolutely superb. The chicken was fragrant and moist, and the rice flavorful. When I finally managed to finish the small chicken I had been given, along with a good portion of the rice, I made the mistake of leaning back, as if finished.

Our host was immediately attentive.

"You need some more chicken, I think," he said.

"Oh, no," I told him. "This is quite enough. It was so big that I am quite full. It was delicious."

"But you Americans eat a lot of food. I am sure you are just being polite."

"Well, perhaps a very tiny bit more, but only because it was so good."

So Chuck and I got second servings as large as the first. We made half-hearted attempts to put some small dent in the piles of food. I mostly just moved things around on the plate. Chuck whispered that the women were watching us eat their food.

Finally, we said that we had enough, that we couldn't eat another bite.

"Is it not to your taste?" the teacher asked us. We protested that it was wonderful and, eventually, he allowed us to convince him that his food was indeed splendid and that we were simply too full to eat even another grain of rice. At that point the women came in and cleared the rug of dishes. We finished with tea and fruit and then it was time to go. Chuck and I thanked the teacher for din-

ner and for his generous hospitality and then we were back on the
dikes, following the boy who now had a lantern to light our way.

The walk home in the warm evening air is probably what kept
me from getting sick. I had eaten more food in one sitting than I
had eaten over the course of a few days.

───────

When we went to work the next day we found out why people
seemed not to like Fucker John.

We were called into the principal's office and asked if we had
dinner at the teacher's house. This was not a good thing for us to
have done. We were told that the provincial governor wanted to see
us. Fucker John, we found out, had ratted us out to the coppers.

There was a young man, the governor's aide-de-camp or something, who showed us out to the patio where the governor sat.
Two armed guards wandered the yard, keeping a careful eye on
me and Chuck, the foreigners accused of bad dining habits. God
only knew what other horrible deeds we were capable of. The governor sat on a desk chair beside the pool, facing away from us as
we came in so that we had to walk around him to get at the two
chairs which had been brought out for us.

If you had chosen the wrong dining companion in, say, California, and were called before the state governor, I think the experience
would be very different. The governor of California is vastly more
powerful than the governor of Laghman Province, but the California
governor's power emanated from his office. It wasn't—isn't—a personal attribute. In the United States, we have gone to great lengths
to depersonalize power. But this guy was powerful because he was
powerful. I don't know what you have to do to become governor of
Laghman, but I am sure it doesn't involve airing really nasty com-
mercials on television or having the guts to hire sleazy, sniveling liars
to spread half-truths about your equally valueless opponents.

This is why the governor of California can't ask me where I have
had dinner and this man could ask me anything he wanted. This
was his province. We were outside troublemakers of no value.

We shook his hand and sat down. He had a contemptuous handshake, as if he knew he had to make a gesture of some sort, but wanted to make it the minimal gesture possible. In the quiet of the courtyard, something dropped from the tree into the pool. Whatever it was disappeared immediately beneath the scummy green surface. Is it a pool, or a pond of some sort? Do Afghans swim? That baffled me. Would the governor take off his astrachan hat, his cloak-like coat, and frolic in the pool as soon as we left? I couldn't picture it.

He didn't say anything. He just looked at us, as if forced to act politely on a state visit to the zoo. "So these animals come from America," you could imagine him thinking. He fished out a pack of K2 cigarettes, shook one loose and fired it up. He smoked it by holding it between his ring and forefingers, making a fist, and sucking at the little hole he left open at the top of his hand. It was fascinating to watch and, of course, made me consider having a cigarette myself. It would show him that we were just two guys, having a smoke by the pool, shooting the bull, straightening out whatever misunderstanding there was about this dinner we went to. I had this idea in my brain for a tiny fraction of a tiny portion of a second.

"The man whose house you went to causes trouble."

This was entirely in Farsi, and a little longer in the original than in this translation. Chuck and I looked at each other, miming absolute innocence.

"We didn't know this."

"It doesn't matter. The man whose house you went to causes trouble. Who else was at the house?"

Suck, suck on the cigarette, staring at us from his ruthless governor's eyes, while his plain-clothed minions swung their nasty little machine pistols around in constant vigilance. Chuck and I were innocents in this, but we sure knew better than to tell this guy anything.

"It was just the teacher and ourselves."

"No one else?"

"No one else."

"And what did you talk about?" he asked.

"Teaching," Chuck said.

"Lessons," I said.

He nodded to himself, smoking his cigarette. He had to use his spare hand to flick the ash when he couldn't shake it off.

"You have to leave Laghman."

We shook our heads. "We are here because the Peace Corps arranged it. We can't leave until the Peace Corps tells us we can leave."

"You have to leave. They will tell you." And then he turned away, looking abstractly at something behind us, off to the side.

Chuck and I looked at each other, then got up and left the courtyard.

Two days later we were back in Kabul.

KHOLM (TASHKURGAN)

GETTING TASHKURGAN

THE ROAD NORTH OUT OF KABUL CROSSES THE HINDU KUSH (Hindu Killer) mountains. Driving, you climbed higher and higher through the Salang Pass, on looping switchbacks etched in a spectacular lunar landscape, forbidding and unforgiving. For long stretches you had to drive through tunnels or through covered roads, which were designed to keep the road clear of snow in the winter and prevent it from being smashed off the side of the mountain by the periodic avalanches. Movement ground to a crawl whenever someone broke down on the narrow, heavily-traveled road, and breakdowns were a routine occurrence. If traffic came to a halt when you were in one of the covered sections, you got to experience a slow version of drowning as more and more of the oxygen was replaced by the carbon monoxide spewed from the trucks and buses.

Although I ended up making this trip numerous times, the covered sections of the road always made me claustrophobic, not so much because the space itself was small, but because the lack of breathable air was so oppressive. Every so often there was a break in the outer wall, letting in some light and providing a glimpse of the gorge. I was always tempted to jump out of the car or bus and slip through the opening so that I could stand outside the tunnel and breathe the fresh mountain air. I never did, because it was not possible to stop without further screwing up the traffic. So I would just try to calm myself into some sort of zen state; as relaxed as possible; taking slow, shallow breaths, covering my mouth and nose with my shirt when I could stand the heat of doing so.

I wondered on each trip if I had run out of luck and would actually die in one of the tunnels, but I always found myself admiring the engineers who had built the road. It must have been an enormous undertaking to carve a road into the sides of these mountains and to blast tunnels through the parts that could not be skirted. The main tunnel alone is three kilometers long. Covering the exposed roads with what amounted to artificial tunnels was a brilliant solution to the problems posed by the terrain and the climate. It was the Soviets, I believe, who built the road. It made me think of the large-scale engineering projects in the U.S. in the early part of the twentieth century.

The Salang Pass was one of the places Chuck and I would consider when we thought of ways to take over the country. Knock out a tunnel or a few of the covered sections and all traffic between the capital and the northern regions would be stopped, probably for months.

It may be impossible to live in Afghanistan without being aware of how easily the unity of the country could be destroyed. The geography itself is divisive, cutting easy communication between the different regions and peoples. The economy is subsistence, which means there is not a lot of trading going on to create bonds between the different regions. So as we wended our way through the mountains, I would see frozen splashes of water sparkling in the weak winter sun, and I would also see tactical military positions: two guys with a rocket launcher in those rocks could hold this pass for weeks. It is a divided, defensive place marked with moments of breathtaking beauty; frozen splashes reaching hopelessly through the thin mountain air being just one small example.

After Laghman, Chuck and I were back in our training house in Kabul, waiting for new assignments. No one was mad at us for having forever closed Laghman to the Peace Corps. Chuck and I had done what we were supposed to do—attempt to integrate ourselves into the community—and everyone knew that this could sometimes backfire. After a few days, we were called back into the office and told what was available.

"There are a number of places here in Kabul," the director told us. He described them to us.

"Anything outside of Kabul?" I asked. I really didn't want to stay in Kabul. Our four weeks in Laghman was not enough to get a sense of living in a remote area.

"There are two places up north," he said. "One is in Pul-i-Khumri and the other is in Kholm."

"Ah, two positions," I said.

"Forget it, John," Chuck said. "Don't even think about it. It won't work this time. I'm going to stay in Kabul."

I almost asked if he was afraid to go up north, but then I looked at him and realized that game was over. So I asked the director if both positions had to be filled or if it was possible to fill just one of them. He wasn't sure, but said there was another volunteer who needed a position and perhaps he would want to go up north.

"Well, I'll go if you can arrange it," I said, and the following week I was driving north in the Land Rover with Marty—the assistant director we suspected of being a spy—and a volunteer I had never seen before. He wasn't a very friendly man, the volunteer. Marty, on the other hand, was a bit of a goofball who slept, I was to find out, in nightshirts.

Pul-i-Khumri was just north of the Salang Pass. It had all the charm and beauty of Laghman. The town was constructed of gray cement and every structure looked to be a uniform height, perhaps ten feet. The center of an Afghan town is the bazaar and it was the bazaars that had been reduced to these storage units. It was depressing. Seeing Afghans operating a bazaar modeled after one of those Stor-It-Yur-Self centers that huddle near freeway on-ramps in the U.S. was like watching lions in the zoo. There was a loss of dignity that seemed almost a violation of human rights.

"Who did this to all these cities?" I asked Marty.

"The king started it," he told me. "He wanted to modernize the country."

Modernize. The word hung in the air as we stood in the dirt and looked around at the farce he had created. You could argue that Afghanistan would be better off modernized: looking, that is, more like Southern California. You could argue—and I would see your point, though it would break my heart to admit it—that the Afghans would be better off with supermarkets than with the charming, but unhealthy, fly-infested, refrigeration-free meat bazaars. You could tell me these people needed real shoes, clothes that actually kept them warm in winter, improved building technology, a better understanding of science as it related to health and agriculture, and I would find it hard to argue.

I don't insist that people remain in a pre-modern world simply because I find it romantic.

But this sort of imposed modernization had no organic basis. The modern world is so full of things that it is easy to mistake the things for the world itself. But if you give people stuff that doesn't grow out of their own experience, they will try to adapt it to their own perceptions—the color-festooned Bedford trucks are a good example of this—but it will never look quite right. And it really won't look right if it's done on the cheap, and that is what happened in Afghanistan.

It looked like Soviet construction. The structures, that is, looked utilitarian, durable, inexpensive, and low-tech. The town center looked as if it had been designed by people who thought that the lack of aesthetic considerations was a sign of hard-headed, pragmatic utility, and that hard-headed, pragmatic utility was a self-evident virtue.

The structures these slab-walled boxes replaced were, admittedly, poorly built. Afghans built brick buildings, but not very well. I have seen Afghans build walls by stacking bricks and then pouring concrete over the pile they had made. The strength of a traditionally-constructed building was in the thickness of the walls, which was at least two, if not three feet. As many of us now know from the media attention given to the country after the terrorist attacks in 2001, Afghanistan is in an area prone to earthquakes, and badly built brick structures are not the buildings best suited to such a region. (Although, drawing on other parts of their history, they do make better shelters during running gun battles than would the largely illusionary Sheetrock walls of suburban American houses.)

Afghans probably didn't think a tremendous amount about aesthetic considerations when they came up with their traditional designs. They built with what they had available, knowing what they knew about construction principles and weather conditions. It is impossible, however, to look at any of their traditionally built structures and not see their beauty. The traditional buildings had lines and proportions that were a delight to look at. And those lines and proportions were dictated by the materials available, the functional demands of the building, and by the builder's interpretations of historical designs. The utilitarian slabs, on the other hand, were designed by accountants to be transported on trucks and lifted by cranes, to be bolted in place to make a market in Laghman, an apartment building in Kabul, or a school in Pul-i-Khumri. Like the square Red Delicious apples which flood our markets because they are more easily packed, these slab-sided boxes provide visible evidence of the limits of modernism.

So I stood in the square in Pul-i-Khumri after meeting with the provincial leaders and thought that I didn't really want to be here. While I would stay here rather than go back to Kabul, it felt like whatever soul was left in this town was buried deep below the bureaucratized modernization and would be difficult to find.

Marty, the other volunteer and I didn't say much as we stood there next to the Land Rover. Finally Marty asked what we thought.

"Well," we both answered, "what's the other place look like?"

"Taskurghan is one of the last places in Afghanistan with a traditional bazaar," Marty told us.

"Let's go take a look at that one."

———

Taskurghan, generally known as Kholm, was on the road to Mazar-i-Sherif, which was one of the northern-most cities in Afghanistan. About a quarter mile before a military checkpoint, we turned off on to a secondary road. We drove about a half-mile along that road, then stopped in what looked like the center of town. We got out carefully because the mud was about a foot-and-a-half deep.

This was a real village. This town hadn't been modernized by some bureaucrat in Kabul sucking relief money out of the Soviet Union. I could almost feel the other volunteer's brain spinning: This was the place. This was why we joined the Peace Corps. Kholm is located on a high plain at the northern edge of a range of mountains. It was a warren of a place, with narrow streets formed by the high walls of the compounds. The only real street was the one leading from the bazaar back to the highway.

And then there was the bazaar itself.

Kholm had, at the time I was there, the last covered bazaar in the country. That's what all the knowledgeable people said when I told them about Kholm: "Why, that's the place with the last covered bazaar in Afghanistan!" Marty had been here before and knew about the bazaar, so he had bypassed the school at which one of us would be teaching and ignored the district office located on one of the side streets, and brought us to this mud puddle at the end of the road.

"Can we walk in this stuff?" I asked him. It looked deep enough to suck us under. I wondered if the Rover would be able to get out.

"Yeah, sure," he said. "You have to see the bazaar."

We walked through the mud, heading toward a dark entryway in one of the buildings. We were careful at first, but after a few steps we had mud inside our shoes and all over our socks and pants, and so we just plowed ahead on the principle that things had already gotten as bad as they could get. A shoe could hold only so much mud, and once it reached that limit, all excess mud fell off of its own weight.

At first the bazaar was too dark to picture, but once our eyes adjusted we saw that there were endless small shops open to narrow streets covered with a wooden roof. Chinks in the roof let in rays and sheets of light, which were blinding in the perpetual dusk of the bazaar. It was a complex maze of a place, and it wasn't until much later that I understood the layout and could walk confidently from one shop to another. Part of the bazaar was built over the river and sections of the clay floor would periodically fall into the rushing stream and anyone walking would have to cautiously traverse the wooden poles that made up the structural bottom of the building.

This was what a bazaar should be like. It was a small, rural version of the Grand Bazaar in Istanbul. Here was romance and excitement. Here were sharp-eyed men huddled over tea, willing to talk with you about that piece of lapis in the display case or that rug over there, the red one with the odd shade of blue on the edges. And when you walked outside there was air so clear you could see the shape of the earth. The roiling of the river was the only sound filling the village, the sky was always a deep blue and the mountains were ever-looming.

We walked through the bazaar, looking in all the shops, and then we went to a teahouse for lunch. Marty yammered on and on, but the other volunteer and I kept our comments to a minimum.

"Isn't this place fantastic?" Marty would ask, poking tentatively at his stew.

"S'okay."

"S'allright."

Marty was put off by our apparent lack of interest, but we had a choice to make. One of us would get Kholm, a place of exquisite beauty, and the other would get that craphole, Pul-i-Khumri. We had to be really careful, because this was a matter of bargaining, of saving face and yet getting what you wanted.

Marty didn't mention the choice until we were back in the Rover, engine running, ready to back out and leave the village. "Oh," he asked casually, "have you thought about which one of you would be here and which would be in Pul-i-Khumri?"

"So you haven't worked out the assignments?"

"No," he said, "I thought I'd let you see both sites and then let you decide."

I was sitting in the back seat; the other volunteer was sitting shotgun. We didn't say a word. The interior of the car was heating up from the whirling of our brains.

The other volunteer finally made a move to begin the negotiations. "Well," he said carefully, drawing out the word, "it doesn't matter very much to me."

I couldn't believe he said that. It was such a bad opening. He was thinking that I would say that it also didn't matter very much to me and then we would inch forward to a decision. But I had already spent my time in an ugly provincial capital and didn't want to do it again, so I bypassed the bargaining and spoke directly to Marty, my tone cheerfully oblivious.

"Gosh, Marty, if it doesn't matter to him, I'd really prefer to stay here in Kholm."

And that's how I came to live in the last village in Afghanistan that had a traditional covered bazaar.

LIVING IN TASHKURGAN

IT WAS THE TWO-STORY HOUSE WITH the blue window frame. Or, it was the two-story house with the green window frame; it depended on whether you were classifying the color in English or in Farsi. The window faced the highway, so when you turned off to go into the town you could see it almost immediately. The house was on the south side of the road and had been built within the last few months over an existing barn.

Except for a few minutes in early spring when a faint haze of green washed over the landscape, the countryside in Afghanistan was unrelentingly brown. And the village was brown as well, with houses constructed of locally produced brick and plastered with something resembling adobe. My sea-green window was a single note of wild exuberance singing out over the harsh rocky land.

"I like the window," I told my landlord. "I like the color."

His leathery face splintered into a broad, bad-toothed smile. "It's green," he said. "It looks good. Next, I will build you a bathroom."

The entrance to my house was outside the compound. There was a narrow alley between the low fence surrounding the hotel and the sheer two-story side of my building. The alley ran from the main road to the dirt road behind the compound, which led out to the village farms. Halfway between the two roads was the entrance to my house, a narrow stairwell that made a sharp right-turn, climbing back toward the main road, and filled the air with the sweet warm smell of hay and horse manure.

At the top of my stairs was the "bathroom." This was just a small room, lightly surfaced with cement to make it waterproof. There was a drain hole about three inches across in the middle of the floor. There was no door, toilet, shower, faucet, bathtub, or basin. My landlord was quite proud of the room and I told him that it was just perfect for my needs. I double-checked when I left: as I suspected, the drainpipe angled out toward the alley, ending in an open pipe sticking out of the wall about eight feet off the ground. Anything going down the pipe would end up on the alley, where I would walk through it on the way to my entrance and then track it back up the stairs. A different sort of Circle of Life.

My room was just past the bathroom. This actually had a door, but there was no way to lock it. Windows faced the highway and the main road into town. It was a beautiful room; light and airy, with thick hand-adobed walls and floor. The ceiling was beamed with long poles, thatched panels forming the surface and keeping mud from the roof from raining into the room. I put the rug from Laghman on the floor. My bed—a pile of thin mattresses—was set up near the window facing the road into town. I used the broad windowsill as a table.

It was getting cold. The mud that Marty and I had walked through on the way to the bazaar was now frozen solid and would stay that way for months. The unpainted walls of my room absorbed whatever heat I could produce from the little woodburning stove. Most of the time that I spent in my room, was on the mattress, under all of my quilts.

Everyone lived in the cold in Afghanistan. This was no different from Kabul in that regard, although outside it was probably colder here. I remember staying at one of the nicer volunteer houses in Kabul on one of my trips to get my monthly pay. I made a cup of tea to drink as I read before sleeping, but I fell asleep without drinking it. When I woke up eight hours later, the tea was frozen solid.

As in Laghman, there were bathroom problems. I stayed in the hotel when I first arrived in Tashkurgan and I continued to use their bathroom after I moved into my new room. They didn't seem to mind this, but it felt increasingly awkward to me. I tried to time this necessity with my job, so that I could use the facilities at the school, and for the most part, that worked.

It was hard to gain complete control over my spoiled Western bowels because periodically I would get food poisoning. One night, reading in my room, propped up on my elbow, and drinking a hot cup of water with sugar (I had run out of instant coffee), I shot bolt upright. I had to go relieve myself now. I scrambled out from under all the quilts, jamming my feet into my shoes and grabbing for my coat and a roll of toilet paper. I picked up my pressure lantern and ran down the stairs. It occurred to me in the seconds it took to scramble down the stairs that the hotel was closed and that I was going to have to go native.

I almost fell on my face vaulting the low fence that separated my house from the large field that surrounded the hotel. Snow. I had slipped on the snow that had accumulated on the fence top. I looked up: snow was coming down in swirling masses of light flakes. I had just managed to pull my pants down around my ankles and get into the proper squatting position when I heard the dogs.

Mastiffs are let free to roam the village at night to keep the wolves away from the sheep, goats, and chickens. The dogs were in hot pursuit of a wolf, and heading toward me. I started waving my lantern in long sweeping arcs in front of me, while holding my pants in my free hand and trying to keep the snowflakes from blowing into my eyes. The animals went piling past me on the other side of the fence, using the narrow alley. The wolf stopped for a minute when it hit the road, turning and feigning an attack on the dogs that immediately backed off, snarling. Then the wolf took off for the center of town with the dogs right on its ass. I waved the lantern for another minute or two, then set it down beside me and concluded my business.

God, I thought, if this isn't a Peace Corps memory, then nothing is.

———

Shit, to put it in its starkest form, was something which occupied a lot of time and thought. There was shit everywhere.
There was shit behind every building and every wall. When buses stopped at a tea house, all the passengers would run around
behind the shop—high-stepping gingerly, looking for a place to
stop—and half the men would drop their pants and take a dump.
The traditional Afghan outfit for men is designed to allow them
to shit in public without exposing themselves.

The winter was the best season when it came to shit because
it froze almost immediately and frozen shit doesn't smell. Ah, but
then Spring would come and four months of frozen feces would
thaw and you'd rediscover your nose as a sense organ.

One freezing cold night I decided that it was just way too cold
to go outside to pee and I thought of the drainpipe in my "bathroom." It certainly saved me a trip outside to Wolf Land, but I
spent the next day heating up water to slosh down the pipe in an
effort to melt the frozen urine. Frozen urine smells exactly like
frozen urine and there wasn't enough air circulation in my little
stairwell-bathroom to hide that fact. Since hot water is a com-
modity that can never be wasted by a Peace Corps volunteer, I
took a sponge bath in my room before running out to the bathroom and throwing the used soapy water down the pipe.

Of course the next time I had to pee in the middle of the night,
I took advantage of the pipe again. By spring, there was a strange,
multi-hued icicle hanging from the pipe opening in my alley.

Late one month I ran out of wood. I waited for the wood caravan to come, but it was late. No one knew why. Sometimes, I was
told, the caravan was late and now was such a time. I asked in all
the small roadside shops if they had any wood to sell, but none of
them did. Increasingly, I would see people standing in the road,
looking out toward the mountains as the wood shortage became
more and more acute. No caravan could be seen.

I left the village to walk into the hills. I thought that it would
surely be possible to find something to burn. I didn't expect much,
but it was better to be cold while walking than to be cold while
sitting in my room. I expected to be able to gather a small collec-

tion of twigs, dried leaves, perhaps small dead plants. I was hoping that I would be able to get enough to have some sort of fire for five or ten minutes. That was my hope.

I walked for hours. I developed theories: the plants must be between the hills, in the ravines, or the plants must be on the lee side of hills, or the plants must be on top of the hills or behind the rocks. I walked. I smoked occasionally. I found nothing.

Nothing. Not very little or nothing of consequence. These hills had been stripped bare a hundred years ago. Two hundred years ago. Ravaged by men, goats, and the ruthless wind until there was not one tiny fragment of anything to burn. I had never seen land like this. You could walk the deserts of Nevada and find something to burn. You could find more to burn on the average beach. But that is fairly meaningless, to say "find more," because to find anything would be to find more.

That night, I burned my blackboard. It made the part of my body immediately facing the stove warm for almost an hour. It was well worth it, although God only knows what inhaling blackboard paint did to my lungs.

THE VISIT

WHEN MELISSA AND CHUCK CAME TO VISIT WE TOOK A CAB TO
Mazar-i-Sherif to have lunch. The cabs waiting at the edge of
town were used more or less as buses, some of them heading south
to Pul-i-Khumri and others north to Mazar-i-Sherif. The drivers of the cabs—black and white Soviet Moskiviches that looked
something like 1957 Fords—would wait until they were full before making the trip to the city. The cars were designed to hold
six people uncomfortably, the way most "six passenger" cars do,
but a full taxicab held eight or nine people, including the driver.
Passengers were spooned into the car, sitting on one hip while facing slightly sideways, sandwiched between two others in the same
predicament. It was extraordinarily uncomfortable after about
half an hour and was made tolerable only because Afghan men,
as far as I could tell, had no body odor.

Whenever I went to Mazar-i-Sherif, my neighbors would tell
me I was putting my life in danger. "Everyone in Mazar-i-Sherif,
Mr. John, is a pervert and a thief."

The bias against homosexuality was quite strong, possibly because it is the only practical sexual outlet for most of the young
men. Marriage was expensive, political, and polygamous and
young men told me they wanted to go to the United States for three
reasons: they could get their own place to live, they would have
electricity, and they could get married. Homosexuality existed in
Afghanistan, but it was hidden so deeply in the closet it could have
been mistaken for the garment industry. Chuck, Ed, and I were

once taken to a gay tea house in Kabul; that had to be one of the oddest experiences I've ever had. There was a transvestite Afghan in drag singing strange, sad, squeaky songs while everyone looked nervously at the door waiting for the cops to burst in.

And then there were all those fat-tailed sheep waddling down the roads with each tail looking like nothing so much as a large, bare ass. The first time I saw one, I burst out laughing, wondering exactly what sort of breeding priorities these shepherds had.

So whenever I headed to Mazar-i-Sherif, I was duly warned against the perversions running rampant in the Big City. As soon as I arrived in the city, I would be asked where I came from.

"Tashkurgan?" the city people would say, shaking their heads. "Everyone in Tashkurgan is a pervert and a thief."

The other thing people in Mazar-i-Sherif asked was whether I was an American. When I admitted to this, I would be told at some length that America was a wonderful place and that the Soviet Union was the spawn of Satan. I didn't know how much to trust this, so I once told some inquisitive people in a shop that I was from Russia. "Oh," they said, and then treated me so poorly I never went back to that section of town. They really did prefer the U.S. to the Soviet Union, even before their civil war started.

On the return trip from Mazar-i-Sherif, Chuck and I were jammed into the back seat of the Moskivch with three other men while Melissa sat in the front seat with an Afghan woman. There was a decent space between the two women and the driver. Melissa sat near the door, directly in front of Chuck. It was a longish drive from Mazar-i-Sherif to Tashkurgan and the woman's husband fell asleep about halfway back, joining the two other Afghan men in a symphony of gentle snoring.

Melissa was whispering nonstop to the other woman, who was covered completely by her chador. Women speak Farsi differently from the men—more of a sing-song cadence—and Melissa was quite fluent. She was teasing and cajoling the woman, but all that we could hear were the tones, higher pitched than her normal voice and something just short of a simper. Melissa turned to us and said, "She's going to show you her face."

We both shook our heads. Chuck hissed out a no. There was actually a law in Afghanistan against non-Afghan men having contact with Afghan women. Melissa said that no one would see.

"Not a good idea, Melissa," I said. "I have to live here."

"It'll just be a peek."

"Don't do it, Melissa," Chuck said.

Melissa whispered some more, then told us that she wanted to see the woman. She was going to look at the woman and set it up so that we could see her as well. I looked over at the husband. Sound asleep. I looked at the driver. If he was aware of any of this, he was a good actor. The woman raised her arm so that Melissa could get the hem of her garment, then Melissa slowly raised it, bunching the chador in her hands until she could see the woman's face through a tunnel of cloth. *Chadari*

"She's beautiful," Melissa said, looking into the little cavern she had created. She leaned in so that her face was against the woman's and spoke with her for a few minutes. Then she started turning the woman's face toward us. "Can you see her?" she whispered, and kept turning until Chuck said yes. Melissa held the chador for another few seconds before letting it fall.

Chuck leaned toward me. "Did you see her?"

"A bit of jawline and part of a nose. Was she pretty?"

He said she was and then we lapsed into silence, wondering if all the snoring was real, wondering if the driver had watched the whole thing in the mirror. We passed the metal gate used to block the highway about a half mile above the village. Marty had visited me once and had rammed the Land Rover smack into the barrier, apparently incapable of seeing the bright red poles blocking the road. The taxi driver swung left at the turnoff leading to the village, the car bouncing and squealing on the rutted dirt road and raising a swirling cloud of dust.

"We have to get out fast," I told Chuck.

"When we stop?" he asked and I nodded. He sat there thinking. "How bad could this be?"

"It depends on how much they saw," I said. "Maybe they'll kill us."

I think Chuck and I were out of the car before it stopped. We were pumped, defensive, waiting for the husband or the driver to come roaring at us. Chuck man-handled Melissa out of the car and pushed her between us. My heart was pumping so much adrenaline through my system that I knew if I didn't hit anyone, it would take a half hour for my muscles to return to normal.

Nothing happened. The driver was counting his money and the three men in the back seat were still asleep. Eventually the driver finished his counting and turned to wake the men. He didn't turn to them and say, "These infidels have gazed upon the naked face of your wife with the help of this American harlot." Instead, he said, "We are here now. You have to get out."

We waited a few more minutes, but there seemed no plan to lull us with non-threatening behavior before getting out the guns, so we all just walked away. Melissa kept telling us that we had never been in any danger, that no one had seen anything.

"But, geez, Melissa," I said. "This is the Ozarks out here. I got in trouble because I talked to one of the progressive women who worked for the school. This woman in the car was wearing a chador and sitting in front of her husband."

"Her sleeping husband."

"That's true," I said. "But next time you do this, at least let me have a look too."

THE FULBRIGHT SCHOLAR

mulberry

I DIDN'T SEE HER AT FIRST.

I ate in this restaurant about four times each week. On the other days, I either didn't eat dinner at all or I ate some sort of snack; piles of pine nuts, for example, or toots (dried fruit). Sometimes, I'd eat peanut butter and nan, if I still had peanut butter left from my last trip to Kabul. In Kholm, we ate Uzbeki nan, a thick, dense, delicious bread with a very slight licorice flavor. I liked the Afghan snowshoe nan down south, as well as the bread baked in the Soviet bread factory in Kabul, but Uzbeki nan was the best bread I've ever eaten.

I entered the restaurant in my usual fashion. I said hello to the two men near the door, whom I had seen earlier in the afternoon in the bazaar. I walked over to the owner, who stood behind the samovar, and we exchanged greetings before I sat down at one of the rickety tables. I shrugged out of my coat, stuffed my hat in one side pocket and pulled a book out of the other. That's when I saw her.

I saw her and thought, My God, I must be getting old because I should have sensed there was a woman in the village before ever leaving my room. To enter and not notice that a Western woman was sitting twenty feet away was a sure sign that some of my senses were in an advanced state of decay.

I knew her vaguely, of course. There weren't that many Western foreigners in Afghanistan. She was one of the two Fulbright scholars from the University of Nebraska. I knew Gail much better, having actually had conversations with her, but this woman had been pointed out to me and we had been in the same rooms at the same times on two or three occasions in Kabul.

The owner brought my tea and asked if I wanted dinner.

"Yes," I told him. "Dinner would be very good." I nodded toward the crazy man a few tables over. "And if my friend wants something to eat, please give him dinner too."

I had eased into buying dinner for the crazy man. At first, I thought he was a relative of the owner. He always sat alone, talking to himself, gesturing to his invisible companions. His clothes were ragged, but he looked reasonably clean, and he never bothered any of the other people in the restaurant. Various customers would point to the crazy man when settling their bills with the owner and it became apparent that they were paying for his tea, for his nan, or for a bowl of stew.

I spoke about this with some of the people at the Peace Corps office in Kabul, to make sure my interpretation was correct; then one night I offered to buy him a bowl of stew.

"That's too much," the owner had said. "Perhaps some nan."

"Yes, that would be good." So I got into the habit of buying him some tea or food, making sure no one else had already made the offer. I didn't buy him something every night, because this man was being supported by many of the people in the village and I didn't want to change the way they did things. It wasn't so much that I wanted to feed this particular crazy man, as that I wanted to shoulder some of my responsibilities as a village resident. After I started contributing, some of the other men would say hello to me when I entered the room. It was well worth the fifty cents that his dinner cost me.

The woman sat at a table near the windows. There were three men with her, local Afghans. Two I recognized and one I didn't, but then I didn't know everyone in Kholm, not even by sight.

It was a dangerous game she was playing. There is a saying in Afghanistan that there are three sexes: men, women, and American women. American women, in this context, included all Western women and the saying indicated that American women lived outside the boundaries that had been drawn between the sexes in Afghan culture.

This perception of Eestern women was based partly, I think, on the way Westerners dressed and interacted. Western women simply looked radically different from native women. Although most resident foreign women dressed modestly by European or American standards, none of them covered their faces in public or hid their hair in any way. Western resident women tended to wear tops that hung low to conceal their hips, but that still left most of their trousered legs free, a sight quite distracting to men not used to seeing such things. The Afghan chador, after all, disguised the entire body, while even very conservative Western clothing made it obvious that women had two legs (separated for their entire length), two arms, breasts, backsides, necks, waists, and all the other attributes of bipedal mammals.

And then there was the way Western women behaved. They behaved the same way Western men behaved! They spoke with confidence. They played softball and loudly commented on bad plays and bad calls. They lived apart from their families. They went out with men and laughed in public.

And, it must be admitted, Western women were overtly sexual. They slept with Western men and they slept with Afghan men. They did this with no effort to conceal what they were doing. Servants in houses with two or three male volunteers had no idea what they would discover when they went to work in the morning. Whom they would discover. I think this overt sexuality fascinated them.

This woman was sitting hundreds of miles from the nearest Western man—not counting me—after dark in a remote village, with three men who in all likelihood had never sat at a table with an unknown woman. This was a violation of everything that had ever happened or been dreamed of in Kholm. It was dangerous. I really wanted to tell her how dangerous it was, but then I figured that she must understand what she was doing. She didn't come all this way to have some patriarchal American try to prevent her from doing what she wanted to do.

And she was ignoring me. The whole place wasn't that big and I had made the social rounds when I entered, so I can assume she saw me. Most likely, she was as surprised to find me there as I was to find her. I knew she was in Afghanistan to study the use of native medicines and that she wandered the country, talking to people in small villages. She was ignoring me, I thought, because she was trying to identify with locals rather than foreigners. So I ignored her.

Ignoring her wasn't easy.

When you are far from home, people from home begin to seem like friends. We begin to think about odd concepts, like "fellow-American" and to say things like, "Wow! I'm from California, too!" This is especially the case when you are in a non-Western country, which gives you more in common with almost anyone from your own country than you have in common with the people in the country in which you find yourself. So it would have been nice to talk with her, show her around my village, and listen to her talk about her research.

But I just read my book and ate my stew. Eventually, the stew was gone and the tea was cold, so I bundled up and went back to my small apartment.

It was a few weeks later that I heard she had died. She had fallen sick, the story went, in some remote area and had relied on local medicines. The medicines had either failed to stem a serious decline or she had been given an overdose . . . the stories varied.

She had been a brave woman.

BEING MEAN TO STUDENTS: PART ONE

THERE IS AN AXIOM AMONG TEACHERS, WHICH IS PASSED ON, AT some point, in all teacher training. It is Don't Smile Until Christmas. This is especially important in Islamic countries, we were told, where teachers aren't supposed to be the students' friends, aren't required to be entertaining, don't have to try to relate to the students' needs, and aren't people who violate any of the role-imposed norms of adult professionalism. (Of course, we were told this by the same people who brought that jackass Rassias in from Dartmouth; the man in Vermont who thought we should rip our shirts off while teaching English.)

We were Americans, so this advice was difficult to follow. In America, a good teacher is entertaining, relates well with students, and violates many of the norms of adult professionalism. The teaching ability of American university professors is determined almost entirely by how well they are liked by their students. Whenever I pass out evaluations in my classes, I wonder if Kant or Hegel were well liked by their students (Kant scares the shit out of me, one student might have said; Expects too much, said another; Hegel's too opinionated, claimed a third). And Socrates would never have received tenure (Constantly badgers the students, lowering their self-esteem and What's with all this walking? Can't we have a room or something?)

Teaching languages requires a lot of interaction with the students. It requires that the students interact with each other. All this interaction among adolescents is difficult to control, so having the

role of the teacher defined in terms of high status and authority
is really helpful. This is especially the case when teaching a language, because the students have to talk in front of their peers and
be willing to accept correction—an experience that no one finds
pleasant. When languages are taught outside the United States,
students talk almost all the time spent in a class. The teacher,
speaking entirely in the target language, begins with a drill of the
previous day's lesson, demonstrates a new construction or part of
language until the students seem able to follow it, then drills the
students on the new material for the remainder of the lesson.

Drilling is fun. You go over something until all the students
in class have had a chance to participate and when you switch
to something slightly new, you make sure you point to one of
the stronger students. Every time a student has to do something
for the first time, you go to a stronger student so that the other
students can hear it being done correctly. If the next student can't
follow what you were doing, you go back to the stronger student
so that he can hear it again.

The problem is that the United States is an individualistic society
and Afghanistan (perhaps Islamic societies in general) is collectivist. This means that Afghans are much more likely than Americans
to engage in what we call cheating. They don't see it as cheating;
rather they figure that if getting the right answer is important, they
would be better off having a short discussion among themselves before answering. (And, of course, they are right.) The Western norm
of individualism—like the Western norm of punctuality—exists
only in the schools and so the students have to engage in some serious gear shifting when they leave home in the morning.

Going to school must have been like daily culture shock for the
Afghan students.

In Kholm, most of my students were about fourteen or fifteen,
but some were at least twenty. This meant they had been stuck
in the seventh or eighth grade for five or six years. While I am
against what critics call "social passing," keeping someone in an
environment in which they do poorly makes little sense. And if
you can remember how mind-numbingly boring your worst high

school course was, imagine taking it for five years. After a while, you don't even pretend.

I included these older students in the lessons to the extent that doing so didn't ruin the class for the other students. We had a truce of sorts: they didn't disrupt the class and I wouldn't bother trying very to hard to make them learn anything.

One day, I entered my eighth-grade class and found that the older students had arranged the chairs around the wood-burning stove in the center of the room. Normally, the students sat at least five feet away from the stove, which created the space that I got to walk around in. The two older students glared at me when I walked in, daring me to respond, while the younger students looked intently at the stove or at the patterns of frost on the windows. There had obviously been a lot of talk among them and they were geared for a fight. I ignored them while I unpacked my bag, took off my hat, muffler, gloves, and coat. I was wearing three shirts, two sweaters, two pairs of pants and three pairs of socks. It was so cold I could barely move, but I had to do something that would both work and yet not damage my credibility.

I turned and looked at the students, keeping my face as blank as possible. I walked all the way around them as they huddled close to the stove. The older students watched me carefully. By the time I got back to the front of the room they were all staring at me. I pointed to my chest. "I am cold," I said. I pointed to one of the older students. "Are you cold?"

He didn't get it. So I repeated it. A younger student whispered something, then whispered it again, more urgently. "Yes," he said, "I am cold."

"*Hub'ass,*" I said. "Good." Then I pulled my chair close to the stove and gave the lesson from there. No one lost face and we kept a little warmer than we would have otherwise. Near the stove, it must have been in the mid-forties.

Whenever I gave an exam, I would go to the teacher's lounge and see who was available to help me proctor. We would make the students sit as far away from each other as possible. All books, notebooks, and bookbags were collected and piled on the floor in the front of the room. My fellow teacher and I would continuously move around the room because the motivation for cooperative behavior (or cheating) was almost overwhelming. On two occasions, we caught students slithering up the aisles on their bellies, trying to get to the books piled so temptingly right in front of them.

The collectivist tendencies created a lack of confidence, I think. The arrogance required to think "I know this stuff, my answer is correct" was rarely found among my students, even among the students who almost always knew their stuff and had correct answers. (In contrast, it is all too common today among my American students, regardless of whether it is justified.) I would ask one of the better students a question in a drill and the class clown sitting behind him would feel obliged to whisper answers, even though he hadn't a clue what was going on. The better student would feel obliged to consider the clown's answer even though he knew that the clown routinely failed exams. This happened all the time, with the result that the good student would change his answer to match that of the poorer student.

When students would refuse to settle down, I would kick them out of class. If I kicked out more than one, I'd have to separate them: You stand right outside the door, you go outside and stand next to the window, so I can watch you. The winter I spent in Kholm was the coldest winter of my life and I would force students to stand outside in the snow, wearing only their cheap plastic sandals and threadbare sport coats over the thin polyester pants and tunic that were the traditional Afghan garb. As I taught, I would see the troublemakers, through the frost-covered windows of my classroom, shivering and stamping their feet.

Baba (uncle) knocked on my door one day after I kicked a boy out into the hall. There was always a man who prowled the halls of the schools and offices and they were all called Uncle. Uncle, get me some tea! or Achmad, tell Uncle I am out of chalk! I went out and talked with him. The student squirmed in the background.

"You can't kick the students out of your class, it teaches them nothing," Uncle told me. "They just goof around outside and disrupt other classes."

"I have to discipline them," I said.

"But this is nothing, what you do. They are losing respect for you." I was never sure if there was a distinction here between fear and respect. My Farsi was not good enough to explore the linguistic nuances of respect and, after all, the meaning of the two words are often blurred in the U.S. among gang members and politicians running for office. So it wasn't just an Afghan thing.

The problem, then, wasn't that I was being cruel to the students, the problem was that I was acting like a softy.

"What is normally done to students who disrupt class?"

"They must be beaten," Uncle told me.

"Oh."

I went to Catholic high school, so I know something of sadistic disciplinary methods. Even when I was in public junior high school in Los Angeles, teachers all had large sticks that they used with great force on our backsides. They called it "paddling," the students called it getting "swats." Eventually, the courts called it "hitting students on the backside with large sticks," and the practice was stopped. Maybe that's what Uncle meant. Maybe I would be forced to whack these miscreants on the ass with a large, flat piece of wood. I might be able to do that, even though I thought it was a huge waste of time and put me in league with all those dysfunctional individuals I despised when I was going to school. My God, I finally might have something in common with the wood shop teacher at Sutter Junior High in Los Angeles, may he rot in hell. It's a good thing I didn't use a mirror to shave.

"And how does one beat the student?" I needed to know the details.

Uncle, a kindly man pushing fifty (which is much older in Afghanistan than in the United States), whirled around and barked at the student to get the sticks. The sticks? What did he mean? "I will show you how the student must be beaten," Uncle said to me, and we waited until the student returned with a bundle of switches. These were tree branches, trimmed smooth, about a third of an inch thick and about three feet long. Baba looked at them carefully, a wine connoisseur perusing his cellar. He pulled one from the bundle and whipped it around. It made a truly frightening noise, hissing through the air like a psychotic snake. Hmm, inadequate, apparently, so Uncle put that back in and tried another. He whipped this one around and was satisfied. (In a far-away galaxy Darth Vader heard the sound and said to himself, "There is a disturbance in the Force.") Uncle gave me the bundle of sticks to hold and I waited for him to ask the student to bend over.

"Come here," he said to the student who had been trying to inch his way backwards into another country. The student took a hesitant step forward and Uncle whipped him across the face. The student raised his arms in defense, which infuriated Uncle, the Master Disciplinarian, who then whipped the student across the legs, trying to get him to lower his arms. These two had met before, it seemed, so the student managed to take most of the beating on his arms. The beating lasted a minute or two and covered at least twenty feet of the hallway as the student retreated and was pursued by his tormentor. I kept my face locked into a hmm-so-that-is-how-one-beats-a-student expression. I thanked Baba for showing me how it was done, and he yelled at the student to bring the switches back to the office.

I needed to think about this, because I wasn't going to beat anyone in this fashion. At the same time, I wasn't going to protest it as barbaric or cruel, because I was just a guy passing through, and undermining their school system seemed outside my job description. I also couldn't send students to Baba for beatings, because then I would lose respect among both students and teachers. It was a real dilemma.

I decided, as an interim strategy, that I would pretend to be a sadistic disciplinarian. I gathered my memories of Father Tona, the Prefect of Discipline at Alemany High School, and went back into the classroom where all the students sat like good boys and girls, minus the girls.

"I have been too easy on you," I said in my meanest voice. They all looked at me. They were absolutely still. The only sound was the occasional crackle of wood in the stove. "From now on, if you disturb the class I will beat you as Baba has shown me." I looked at all of them, one at a time, the silence deafening. "I will beat you harder, because Baba is old and I am stronger."

They sat there, afraid to look at me and afraid to take their eyes off me. "You have made me look bad," I said. "And you WILL NEVER MAKE ME LOOK BAD AGAIN! Is that clear? IS THAT CLEAR?"

It was clear.

The student who had been beaten was eighteen or nineteen years old. He was bigger and stronger than Baba. In America, I remember thinking, an eighteen or nineteen-year-old would not have tolerated such a beating. The beatings delivered by the priests in my high school had an aura of symbolism about them: the student was bent over, a thick belt or paddle was used. Baba had whipped the student in a way that looked like an attack, in a manner that could have seriously hurt the student, who was allowed to protect himself to some extent. It looked, that is, something like a fight.

It required tremendous social pressure to keep this system from falling apart. You could pull it off to some extent in Catholic schools because priests—at least until all the recent allegations of misconduct—had a status that was difficult to question. In Army basic training, drill sergeants could do things that would not be tolerated from anyone else. But that was about it.

I remember thinking, as I gave my I-am-Baba speech to my class, how sorry I felt for the boy who had been beaten. He sat near the windows, humiliated. He had just been treated like a small child or as a balky animal, and it burned in him. He was a man, not a boy, and yet was forced to stay in school, and so he reacted against it. He was a man, not a boy or a balky animal, and he should have pulled the stick from Baba's hand, snapped it in two, and walked out of the building.

I remember thinking as I gave the little speech, I am such a liberal. Then, I am such an American. Don't tread on me, Baba.

DREAMING OF WATER

I DREAMED OF WATER. BURIED DEEP UNDER ALL OF MY QUILTS, wearing almost everything I owned, I could hear the flow of water over rocks. I heard it all night long.

I dreamed of swimming, of fording rivers, of sailing skiffs. I watched waterfalls, stood in torrential rainstorms, and sank slowly into deep, still pools.

In my dreams I was almost always naked, as one should be when water is involved, and the water flowed in sheets across my body.

I must have been completely dehydrated.

I decided that I would go to Greece when I left Afghanistan. I would go to the Greek islands and lie in the Mediterranean sun, with the sea lapping at the shore and large bottles of water close at hand. Water and nudity were the two things lacking in my life.

I began to think about this all the time and, after a while, it became a fact: that I would go to Greece became as certain and as real as if I had already gone, the future had collapsed into the past. I thought I would leave this country, shedding my clothing as I went, discarding the restrictions of being the polite foreigner in a confined society, and walk into the water until it closed over my head.

KISSING IN THE HALLWAY

"YOU SHOULD COME DOWN THIS WEEK," THE DIRECTOR SAID. "We need to talk about this letter you've written."

I was standing in the district office in Kholm, talking on the phone, surrounded by people watching me talk. It's their phone, I thought, surely they've seen people use it before.

"Does it have to be this week? Why not wait until the first of the month, so I can pick up my pay at the same time."

There was a longish pause. "Your letter sounded somewhat urgent."

"Oh, I was mostly bored when I wrote that," I told him. "I just thought you should know what's going on up here."

"So you are willing to wait?"

"Sure. It's not that big a deal."

"Okay. Next week then."

"Let's make it Friday, so I don't miss class."

There was a little more chatting, then we hung up and I gave the phone back to the secretary I wasn't supposed to talk to. I didn't look at her while I did it. Instead, I looked at the male teacher standing off to the side. I held the phone at one end with my fingertips so that she could take it from me with plenty of visible plastic between our two hands. A few weeks back, I had been told that I wasn't supposed to talk to Afghan women. When it became obvious that I had no idea what the district supervisor was talking about, he said that a complaint had been made by some teachers who had seen me talking with the secretary while I was running the mimeograph machine. I think I had said flirty things like Is this where you keep the paper? and Well, I'm done now.

I had been bored when I had written to the director. I think I had run out of things to read, or re-read, or re-re-read. By the hideously bright light of my pressure lamp, I wrote a long essay telling the Peace Corps office that there really wasn't a job here. I taught two forty-minute classes three times a week. In between, I wandered the hills and hung out in the bazaar. Tacked on to the end of the essay were eighteen reasons why no one should stay in Kholm.

What I didn't tell them was that my brain had gradually ground to a halt. I found this a little alarming.

I had been under the impression that I could become amazingly creative and insightful if left alone. It was a romantic ideal, but it didn't work for me. I wrote letters about the books I was reading in order to somehow make them mine, to integrate the ideas into my head. But, except for these imaginary, one-sided conversations, I really had no one to talk to. And, with no one to talk to, I began to lose the voice in my head so that after a while I didn't even have myself for company. I noticed I was losing long stretches of time.

I had become a member of a group that spent some part of each day in a small shop, drinking tea. I would wander down the corridor in the bazaar after finishing my classes and be greeted by a group of men sitting on a deep earthen shelf at the back wall of one of the stores. The number of men on the shelf ranged from three to six, sometimes seven, not counting me. I would be invited to sit with them and they would move around until there was a place to squeeze in, then they would throw a blanket over our legs to keep us warm. On really cold days, we'd pull the blanket up so that only our shoulders, faces, and the hand needed for drinking tea was exposed . . . the right hand, of course, since the left had been designated for other duties, as discovered in the Tehran airport.

What surprised me was how little these men talked.

"It is very cold today," I would say.

"Yes, it is."

"Colder than yesterday."

"Yes, even colder."

Then we would sit in silence until my tea arrived.

"Oh, here is your tea."

"Good. The tea will warm me up."

I expected gossip or conversation, but mostly they were just comfortable sitting in silence. I sometimes teach a course in the history of journalism and I tell the students that the reason tiny villages in Colonial America didn't have newspapers was because they didn't have any news. Everyone knew what was going on, and there wasn't very much going on.

Kholm was stuck in two political systems; a centralized, vaguely socialist government supported by military power and a residual feudal system in which someone could claim to own the village. Neither of these creates a social culture conducive to gossip. There wasn't any dating, divorce, or noticeable hanky-panky going on. There weren't any televisions, radios, or newspapers to introduce scandals and controversies from far away. When the nomads came to town, they stayed carefully separate.

So we just sat there. I remember two moments of excitement. Once, the shopkeeper sent the boy out for some sugared almonds to go with our tea. When the bag got passed down to me, I noticed that the small sack had been made from an English language magazine. I started reading it, turned the bag around and saw a photograph of Bertrand Russell, the British philosopher who died in 1970. It was so shocking to see this man's face while sitting cozily in the Middle Ages that I said, "I know this man!"

They all leaned in and I showed them the photograph. "It's Bertrand Russell," I said. "He's a famous teacher in England." Evidence of my planet: I didn't just fall from the sky.

"Is he your friend?" one of the men asked me.

"No, I've never met him."

"Is he a friend of your family?"

"No," I told them. "He is just someone I read about in school."

"Oh, so you don't know him."

"Well, he's dead now. He died a few years ago."

"You didn't know him and now he's dead." He shook his head.

"It's too bad you didn't meet him before he died," said another.

"Yes," I said. "It is too bad."

"Can you pass the candy to me?"

"Yes, of course. I am sorry." I took one last look at Russell's bony English face and then passed the bag to the man on my left. I knew more about Russell than I knew about anyone in Afghanistan. I knew about his ideas, his dry humor, his elitist attitudes, his courageous political stands, and his strange British philandering. I knew about his grandparents and his parents. I knew about many of his students. But this sort of knowing meant nothing here: I didn't know him, really. I knew of him. It occurred to me that Russell, who was one of the founders of analytic philosophy, would have appreciated this distinction.

I never liked Russell very much anyway.

The second event that stands out in that long period of sitting was when the men I sat with tried to effect a reconciliation between two old friends. Twenty years ago the two men had had a falling-out over the sale of a horse and had not spoken since. Both men, however, hung out in this shop; taking care to pass by if the other had arrived first.

"We told Achmad that Tusupbekov would not be here today, but we invited him."

"They must talk. It's been too long."

Tusupbekov showed up first and looked distinctly unhappy. I asked him about the horse.

"It was lame," he said, mimicking lameness, since my Farsi didn't run to these sorts of words. "But not when I sold it to him! It was fine when I sold it to him. It was a good horse."

"But Achmad thinks you knew it was lame."

Tusupbekov pulled himself up to his greatest height, about five foot six. "I am a Khazak," he said. "I do not lie about horses!"

"A what?" I asked.

"A Khazak," someone said.

"Where are Kazakhs from?" I asked him.

"They are from Kazakhistan, in Russia." Afghans called the Soviet Union Russia, which they pronounced as rooo-she-ah, with three syllables.

Then it dawned on me. "You're a Cossack?"

"Yes. A Khazak."

I fairly gushed over him. It was like meeting a member of the Roman Legion, an English longbowsman, or a Mayan. Cossacks were a fierce people who rode small ponies and slaughtered thousands of innocent people in an outpouring of enthusiastic ignorance and xenophobia. The stuff of which legendary heroes are made. While I was telling him how impressive it was to meet an actual Kazakh, Achmad arrived.

Achmad took one look at Tusupbekov and said something sharp and harsh that had the same nonverbals as "what kind of bullshit is this?" has in English. He then stormed down the corridor, going deeper into the bazaar. Immediately, the group splintered. Half the men took off after Achmad, who broke into a trot, and half grabbed Tusupbekov and dragged him in their wake.

It was the most fun I had had in months. Everyone was yelling. Achmad wanted everyone to leave him alone and everyone in his group was telling him he was stubborn and unwilling to listen. Tusupbekov was losing interest in the whole plan and so we really had to hold on to him to keep him with us; he was whining and protesting while we were wheedling and pushing. We swarmed all through the bazaar and finally got Achmad cornered in the small room where the two main corridors of the bazaar met. We were all huffing and puffing by this time and we forced the two old friends to stand on one side of the little mud platform that was in the center of the room. We all lined up around the walls.

"Give him a hug!"

"Shake his hand!"

"Tell him you're still friends!"

We were all yelling at them while they stood inches apart, glaring at each other. Finally, the shopkeeper took two steps toward them and pushed Achmad into Tusupbekov. They wrapped their arms around each other, in the most perfunctory way imaginable, then gave each other a kiss. We all cheered at the magic we had wrought, then went back to the shelf in the shop, sat down, and called for more tea. We were completely satisfied with ourselves.

It had been a wonderful day.

————

"You have too many reasons," Marty said. "Somebody helped you write this."

"What?" That made no sense at all. "Why would I need help writing a letter?"

"You have too many reasons, that's all." He shook his head. "Eighteen."

We talked about that for a while. This conversation was not going well. The director and the assistant director seemed very disturbed by the letter. I didn't understand their reaction. It was just grumbling, for the most part. Once the director realized I wasn't suicidal from isolation, he pretty much lost interest in me, but Marty was incensed.

"You know what?" Marty asked. "I think you're just horny."

I burst out laughing. "Jeez, Marty! Of course I'm horny! I said in the first part of the letter that I was horny. I said I didn't mind not getting laid, but I had to have a reason for it. If I had a job, I'd think that, even though I wasn't having any sex, I at least had something to do. But in Kholm, I just don't have any sex. I tell you, it's hard to think that pretty views of the mountains make up for that."

Marty exploded. I didn't know anything about the culture, he said. I hadn't made any effort to make friends. I just hadn't bothered to try to fit in.

"Well, Marty," I said, "that just isn't true."

The director realized we weren't getting anywhere and suggested we meet again the next day. We left the director's office and that's when the second miracle of my stay in Afghanistan took place.

The director's office was at one end of a T. We walked the short distance to the main hallway with Marty lambasting me for failing to become acculturated. When we turned the corner, he really got into gear and I became a symbol of some giant generic failure. I hadn't made any friends, he yelled, and I made no effort to understand life in this country. While he was yelling, a tall Afghan man walked toward us, wearing a Nuristani hat, with a long blanket thrown over his shoulders. I watched him, blinded somewhat by the afternoon sun shining off the floor, and listened to Marty rant.

"John, John!" The Afghan called out, extended his arms wide in greeting, and quickened his pace toward us. It was Mahmood, from my school in Kholm. I held out my arms and we gave each other a huge hug.

"I told you I would come to see you in Kabul!" he said to me in Farsi, and gave me a big wet kiss, smack on my lips. This is the way Afghan men greet their friends.

"It is so good to see you, my friend," I told him. "You have no idea how good it is to see you."

We turned to face the director and Marty. Mahmood had a great grin on his face. Marty just stared at me.

"I think John has a friend visiting him, Marty," the director said. "We should continue this tomorrow."

I introduced everyone, and then Mahmood and I walked, hand-in-hand, up the hallway and out of the building. I could feel Marty's baleful glare the whole way.

At the meeting the next day, there were no references to fitting in or having friends. Instead, we talked about consolidating the two northern positions, letting me return to Kabul.

KABUL, THE SECOND TIME

GIRLS IN THE RAIN

IT WAS RAINING, WHICH IS UNUSUAL IN AFGHANISTAN. MY apartment was located in the neighborhood of the Peace Corps office in Kabul, so it was about a twenty-minute walk to Chicken Street. I was going to Tritoni's, just off Chicken Street, to get a cafe au lait.

Tritoni's was Kabul's answer to Bogart's Rick's. It was an odd place, a place to get coffee and gelatto in a country in which everyone drank tea, and refrigeration was unheard of. The owner was a graceful gladhandler of a man who talked with all of his customers, moving from table to table, occasionally sitting briefly and joining in a conversation, his eyes always scanning the restaurant to make sure everything was going as it should. The restaurant—both inside, and outside in the courtyard—was always filled with a wonderfully eclectic group of people, mostly foreigners. There was Charles, from Cambridge, Massachusetts, who wandered the country buying rugs and wearing his father's old felt hat. Charles ended up in prison for a while, after the Communists came into power. And there was Robert, the bushy-bearded man from Berkeley, a sort of hippie entrepreneur, who exploited the low wages and manual dexterity of Afghan craftsmen, and his wife, affectionately known as the World's-First-Pregnant-Woman after her one topic of conversation. As a gesture of solidarity with the people she was exploiting, she decided to have her baby naturally, in a country with the second lowest life expectancy in the world. And, of course, there was always a motley collection of

115

Peace Corps volunteers like me, hanging around on the look-out for the random tourist and wanting to speak English after another day in Afghanistan.

So I was going to Tritoni's in the late afternoon and it was raining softly, a heavy blowing mist that made no sound as it washed into the windows and across the sidewalk. I avoided most of the rain by walking under a small overhang on the row of shops that lined the street. I was ambling—there is no reason to hurry in Afghanistan—with my hands in my pockets, thinking that it had been a number of days since I had seen any Americans. I had been here almost a year at this point so I knew that the girls who were walking toward me under the overhang would have to step out in the rain: I was, after all, a man.

As a Peace Corps volunteer, I was expected to respect local cultural norms rather than impose my own. This meant that as these young women got within a few paces of me, I should stifle my culturally-imposed desire to step out into the rain in order to let them continue under shelter. One of my students could be watching, I thought, and I would lose all credibility. Being sexist and inconsiderate could, in this instance, be seen as a moral imperative.

Afghan women are invisible. Men, especially foreigners, are not supposed to look at them, and the women are concealed from head to toe by their chadors. They walk the streets wraith-like, floating by on invisible feet, and after a while you simply don't see them anymore. They are the opposite of the Emperor's New Clothes.

Still, at some level, you notice them because I knew, for example, that these were young women rather than middle-aged or elderly women. It was the way they moved, perhaps, or that they were holding hands through the damp material of their chadors. And chadors aren't raincoats: a woman in the rain in a chador is one of the saddest sights you can see.

I was thinking all this with the part of my brain I could largely ignore while I wondered if my friend Chuck would be at Tritoni's. It was because of this, and because they were, after all, girls, and it was, for pete's sake, raining, that as the girls approached me, I stepped into the rain to let them pass. It was an automatic thing, a knee-jerk reflex.

But as I passed them, the first girl slammed me with a hip block that knocked me out into the middle of the sidewalk, her friend gasped in shock as she did it. I turned to look at her, at them. Two girls covered completely in yards of damp fabric, eyes hidden behind the woven grills, and me, standing in the rain, all of us shocked into silence. And then we started to laugh, bending over at the absurdity of it. The girl in the green chador, the one who bumped me, snorted loudly which made all of us laugh even more. I told her, in Farsi, that it was nice meeting her. She laughed and said hello, then her friend gave her a push, and they walked away.

She knew what I had been thinking, the girl in the green chador. She knew, even as I stepped out into the rain to let her pass, that I had completely discounted her as a human being. She knew this and so she interjected a bit of vaudeville into downtown Kabul, letting me know that she was under there. Under all that fabric. Under all that bullshit.

A week or so later, I was walking down that same stretch of sidewalk, heading home. It was late and Kabul at night can be quite dark. It was rare to see people walking at night, but there was someone walking toward me. My first impression was that it was a very tall man. This is odd, because except for the Nuristanis, Afghans are not very tall people. But you don't see Nuristanis all that often in Kabul. Then I noticed that the person was really tall—like abnormally tall—and so I tried to get a better look at this man. Unfortunately, the light was very bad. There was a street light behind me, one in the middle of the block—halfway between us—and one behind the man walking toward me. This made him very hard to see. Mostly, I got the basic human silhouette: biped, taller than wide, walking erect. I saw two legs, so I knew it was a man rather than a woman . . . plus it would have been extremely unlikely that a woman would walk alone at night. But there was something wrong with this image.

He looked abnormally tall—well over six foot—yet his head was either as wide as his shoulders or he didn't have a head at all. Plus, he was (I'm not sure how to say this) wavy at the edges. And bouncy.

We were closer now, but still all I could see was a shape back-lighted by the street lamp. Whatever was coming toward me had six arms and no head. The arms were of different lengths and moved in a swimming motion. I slowed down and considered crossing the street. I considered—briefly, to my credit—whether it would be unmanly of me to wet my pants and run screaming in the opposite direction.

My brother and I once saw an optical illusion as we drove on a rural highway north of Los Angeles. The mountain on our left, across a narrow valley, seemed to be moving at tremendous speed. I remember my brain just stopping: I had no category for this. My brother, who was driving, followed my slack-jawed gaze and drove off the road. He too didn't have a category that allowed for moving mountains. That was how I felt walking straight at this Shiva-thing coming toward me: I had no category for this. Perhaps my time had just run out, perhaps this was fate; payback for all my bad behavior or for mocking the gods on such a continuous basis. Perhaps the FBI or some has-been actor from *Believe It or Not* would be able to use a footprint-following machine and be able to trace me to the middle of this block, at which point the footprints would stop and all knowledge of me would cease. This was it, I guessed, as I walked toward my fate: Sumser met a monster on the way home from Tritoni's. Damn.

It got to within ten feet of me, waving all six arms, then stepped into the circle of light thrown by the lamp in the middle of the block.

"Hello," I said.

"Hello," he replied. "Are you good?"

"Yes, I'm good. Are you good?"

Then he disappeared behind me and I walked another block before turning right and going down the street to my apartment.

A goat is about as large as a good-sized dog. Even after a goat's been decapitated, eviscerated and skinned, it is heavy and awkward to carry. The man who had been walking toward me had decided to slip the goat's carcass over his head . . . to wear it rather than carry it. He had stuck his head into its ribcage so that the torso of the animal rode above his head and the legs stuck out to the side, moving in rhythm to his walk.

Shiva or this guy. Hard to tell which was stranger.

THE MORNING PARADE

THERE IS A PART OF KABUL THAT CONSISTS OF HIGH-RISE SOVIET housing. The buildings were put up using some sort of pre-fab concrete slab construction and when you put all those words together—pre-fab, slab, concrete, Soviet—you get a good idea how attractive they were. They were utterly without charm. At that point in my life, I had not yet been to Athens, another city ruined by utilitarian construction methods. These buildings in Kabul looked like American housing projects, and had been placed on the landscape with absolutely no regard for the culture or the surrounding buildings.

I rode my bicycle through this area on my way to work at the technical school. Generally, there wasn't very much traffic or people in the area, but one day there were hundreds of people lined up four abreast, lines of women and lines of men. They were in a side street that paralleled the main street (which never made much sense to me). The men were on one side of the street and the women were on the other, and everyone was wearing a red kerchief or holding a small red flag. Obviously, I thought, there was a holiday that I wasn't told about, and it looked as if there was going to be a parade.

I waved to a few of the men who were hanging about between the two lines of people and they waved back, so I turned to the right so that I was riding between the men and women. It was a glorious morning, warm and bright, and the patches of red were dazzling in the early spring sun.

Five or six of the men broke ranks and surrounded me, holding the bicycle so that I didn't fall down. They were so tightly packed around me that I couldn't put my feet on the ground. I sat on the bike, with my feet on the pedals, and said hello, how are you doing? Is it a holiday today?

"Yes," one of them said to me. "It's a holiday, but you cannot be here."

"Oh, I'm sorry," I said. "You all looked wonderful, lined up, and I wanted to see."

"That's fine, but you have to leave now."

"Okay. If you let go of me, I'll ride away."

He shook his head. "You can't go that way." Meaning I couldn't continue to ride between the lines of men and women.

"Then I'll turn around." I felt really stupid, disrupting their celebration. I pointed back the way I had come. "I'll go that way."

Then all the men picked me up, on the bicycle, and carried me through the line of men to the main street. The lines of men parted in that odd silence that Afghans use when they are coordinating an activity. It was such a strange experience that I wasn't quite sure how to respond, so I thanked them as if carrying me off, vehicle and all, was a normal way of changing directions. I shook their hands and left, heading toward the school. The whole thing had not lasted longer than two or three minutes, but I felt absolutely wonderful for the rest of the day: the bike ride, the glorious weather, the friendly camaraderie of the men in the parade combined to make one of the many perfect mornings I experienced in Afghanistan.

Later that evening, I was told it had been the May Day parade, and that the men and women lined up along the street were members of the Communist Party who were preparing to march in protest against the United States Embassy.

SPIES LIKE US

JANE WAS AN AMERICAN TRAVELING ALONE. SHE WAS TALL, blond, beautiful, and fun to talk with. Her only flaw, as far as I could tell, was that she seemed to be attracted to Chuck.

I was in Tritoni's when she came in and sat in my booth. There weren't a lot of tourists in Afghanistan and most of the ones we saw were on their way to India or, having been in India, were heading back to Europe. There were exceptions, of course: Robert and his ever-pregnant wife, for example, here to colonize the craftsmen, and Charles, the rug dealer. They came and stayed, but such people were rare.

Even in those relatively peaceful days, Afghanistan was not the most hospitable of holiday destinations. There was a man bicycling from Europe to India who had been killed camping in the mountains. He had been killed by bandits, we were told and we all looked at one another: bandits? And two Australians had been found skinny-dipping in one of the rivers and were murdered for their outrageous behavior. I remember thinking that skinny-dipping in Afghanistan was on par with trying to conduct a Satanic mass in the Vatican: don't be surprised if the mob tears you to pieces. And don't be surprised if it's Aussies who are getting in trouble, wandering the world in their khaki shorts and eating cheese wherever they go, oblivious to the locale except as a form of playground. They were far worse than Americans who, if anything, were overly sensitive to cultural norms, since they tended to be on voyages of enlightenment.

And there were women like Jane.

Jane was just wandering. She was smart enough to know how to blend in when that was important—and it took some doing for a tall blond woman to blend into the crowd in Afghanistan. She had rented a room just off Chicken Street, about half a block from Tritoni's.

She had been in the country for almost two weeks when she sat down at the table. I am not sure why I started talking to her the way I did. Partly, I suppose, I didn't know why she was interested in Chuck when Chuck's mind was elsewhere and I was obviously unattached. And partly I was just feeling mischievous.

"Hi, John," she said as she slid into the booth.

"Hey, Jane." She was really pretty. Have I mentioned that? She was almost as pretty as Gail, the Fulbright scholar, but Gail was never in town.

"Have you seen Chuck?"

Chuck, I knew, was with Kay, the Peace Corps nurse. Kay was taking her two children somewhere and Chuck had tagged along. "He's with Kay," I told her. "They went out of town someplace."

"They seem to be pretty good friends," Jane said.

"Yeah, well, Kay is really great. We all . . ." I almost said, "We all like Kay," but then I decided not to. A tiny piece of an idea had crept into my brain. Chuck was seeing someone, but Jane didn't know her, and as much as I would have liked to tell this to Jane, there was the Code of the West which had as one of its cardinal rules never to sabotage the romantic interests of your friends. This rule was right after the one saying you should never kick a man when he's down and just before the admonition always to sit with your back to the wall when playing cards in a saloon. But Jane was extremely pretty—which has been both the weakness and the rationale for the Code of the West—and it occurred to me that I couldn't be held responsible for conclusions she drew from things I didn't tell her.

That's the idea that started this whole episode.

"What?" she asked. "We all what?"

"Oh, nothing," I said with greatly exaggerated nonchalance. Then I changed the subject. "So, what are you doing today?"

She looked at me without saying anything. She knew I was acting oddly, but she didn't know why. I fumbled a bit with my coffee cup, a liar hiding his nervousness. I kept trying to look her in the eyes, but then let my glance slide off to one side. Generally, creepy behavior.

"What's wrong, John?"

"Nothing," I said. "Chuck and Kay are just sight-seeing, that's all. Don't go jumping to any conclusions."

"I'm not jumping to anything," she said. "Why would I jump to a conclusion?"

"Right, no reason at all. So, big plans for today?"

"No plans for today. You sure are acting strangely."

I leaned forward over the table. "Look, Jane. Just back off, okay?" I said this forcefully, in a voice barely loud enough to cross the table. "This has nothing to do with you, so let's just talk about today and about what you've been doing the last few days. Chit-chat. Let's just do that."

She shook her head. "What is wrong with you?"

I started packing up my stuff. I had been writing a letter when she sat down. "I think I'd better go," I said. "This is just bullshit and I can't deal with it." I was moving slowly; surely she would stop me.

She put a hand on my arm. "Don't go," she said. "I don't know why you're mad at me."

I sank back in my seat, heaving a huge sigh and sat staring at the ceiling, then I closed my eyes. I stayed this way for about two minutes. I felt her looking at me, wondering what was going on. Then, leaning forward and catching her eyes, I told her I wasn't mad at her.

"It's not you," I said. "There's been a lot going on recently and there are some things that it just isn't important to know about. That you really shouldn't even think about."

"Like what? I don't know what you're talking about."

"Like me and Chuck and Kay, for example. You should leave this alone. Stop poking around in it."

"I'm not poking around. What's there to poke around in? Two Peace Corps volunteers and a nurse. What's the secret?"

"Exactly," I said. "No secret at all: just two Peace Corps volunteers and a nurse." She was looking at me intently and I met her gaze, then let my eyes slip guiltily to the side. "Really, that's all it is. Just keep thinking that."

"I thought we were friends."

"We are friends, Jane. It's just that this is none of your business and if you keep messing about in it, people can get hurt." I looked around as if trying to plot an escape. "I'm going to get another coffee." I stood up, walked a few paces, then turned around and, very pointedly, picked up the spiral notebook I had been writing in and put it in my pocket. "Do you want anything?"

This would only work because Jane was smart. She would try to read between the lines of the bullshit I was feeding her and she would end up thinking the only thing that would make sense of my convoluted ramblings.

"I get it," she said when I sat back down.

"Really?" I asked. "You know, I went out to the base of the mountains last week, to look at the wall. Have you been there? I have been thinking of climbing it."

She leaned way across the table and whispered, "You're spies, aren't you?"

I looked shocked. "What makes . . ." I started to bluff, then stopped, letting a long pause draw out. I put a rough tone into my voice and asked her who she had been talking to.

"No one. I haven't been talking to anyone."

"Then why would you say that?"

"It's the only thing that makes sense."

"I don't believe you. This is the same damn thing that happened in South Af..." I cut it off.

"South Africa? You were in South Africa?"

"Will you keep your goddamn voice down?"

"What happened in South Africa?"

"Have you ever noticed that Chuck can't hear out of one ear?" I tried to sound bitter. "There was an explosion. Too many people talking about things that were none of their business." Chuck had just finished Ranger training back in the States, years earlier, and was clearing out his area, getting ready to ship out to Vietnam. He tossed some junk into a trashcan that one of his fellow trainees had booby-trapped and that was the end of Chuck's military career.

Jane thought about that. I took out my notebook, made a quick marginal notation in my letter to one of my brothers, then slapped it closed and put it back in my pocket.

Jane said, "So you are spies."

I laughed. "I think that's a word only used in Hollywood, Jane. We look at stuff, figure things out that's all. It's not a big deal." I lowered my voice even further. "Of course my pen shoots tiny cyanide pellets and there's a radio in the top button of my shirt."

She laughed nervously.

"Then who do you work for?"

I shook my head. "Jane, come on. We work for the Peace Corps." I did everything but wink. I would have winked, but the best I can manage is a sort of lop-sided blinking. I thought about laying my finger along side my nose, but figured that might be a little over the top.

"Ah," she said, nodding. "Of course you do."

"Of course we do. And should anyone ever ask . . . ?"

"You all work for the Peace Corps."

I worked on my coffee for a few minutes. Jane looked lost in thought. "What about Larry," she asked. "Does he know his wife is a spy?"

"I wish you'd stop using that word," I said. "This is really hard to talk about because you aren't supposed to know any of this."

"But I do know," she said.

"I know. That's what makes it hard. Let me think for a minute. I need to sort out what I can and can't say." I looked down at the table, deep in thought. I was wondering when Chuck would be back because I really had to tell him this before he ran into Jane. I would go by his house on the way back to my apartment. I looked up. "What was your question?"

"I wanted to know if Larry knew about his wife's, uh, activities."

"Do you know what Kay's son's name is?"

"Chuckie," she said and I let her stew in it. Then she said, "I don't understand."

"Larry's just a guy who works at the embassy."

"Oh my God!"

"Yeah. It's an amazing world."

"So Chuck and Kay . . ."

"Yes."

"And where do you fit in?"

"I work with them."

It went on like this for quite a while. She wanted to help, if she could, so I told her about our communication system. A specific shoe shop in the main bazaar was our link with a key informant. We had to check the fifth pair of shoes on the second shelf from the top every second day to see if a note had been stuffed into it. The message would be placed there before ten o'clock, if at all, but the problem was that I increasingly suspected that I was being tailed.

"Can't you lose them?"

"Oh, sure, that isn't difficult, but then they know I lost them and they get even more suspicious. It's becoming tricky."

"I could check for you."

I shook my head. "We can't allow you to get involved. You already know way more than you should."

"But I go to the bazaar almost every day. I could do it for you."

I was reluctant, but I let her talk me into it. If it looked at all peculiar, I told her, then she'd have to abort. I actually said "abort." She agreed to check the following morning and a day or two after that, I'd meet her at her room to see if a message had been placed in the shoe.

I left at that point because it wouldn't do for us to be seen together, what with her new involvement in our activities. I found Chuck and told him the whole story. Chuck told Kay, Kay told Larry. Kay told me the following day that Larry thought he needed a bigger role.

It was probably three days later that I finally had the time to find Jane. I knocked on her hotel room door. She opened the door and, as soon as she saw it was me, she walked back into the room without saying anything. I followed her in, letting the door close behind me.

"I know you were making up all of that spy business."

"Oh."

"I was talking with Chuck and he told me."

"Oh," I said again. "Exactly how pissed off are you?"

"I was really mad when he told me, but it was funny, so it was hard to stay mad. I guess I'm not mad at all, except it makes me so mad that you did it to me."

"Okay." I didn't know what to say.

"I can't believe I went to the bazaar."

"So was there a note in the shoe?" I asked, then started to laugh.

She laughed, too. "There was some paper wadded up in the toe. I guess there's always paper wadded up in the toes. But I went to this unbelievable amount of trouble to steal this old crumpled piece of newspaper and until I talked to Chuck, I thought it must have been in code or something."

"Did you keep it?"

"I just threw it away this morning, when I was still mad at you."

"Would it help if I bought you some coffee at Tritoni's?"

"Not coffee," she said. "I want an ice cream."

So I bought her an ice cream and we talked for an hour or so. The next day she left for Turkey.

BAMIYAN

NOT LONG AFTER WE TURNED OFF THE MAIN HIGHWAY ON TO the secondary road, the small bus pulled into a village so that the drivers could gas up and we could get something to eat. The village was a jumbled pile of buildings in the crook of a river, the dusty center full of trucks and buses; loading and unloading, spewing smoke and grinding gears as they trundled back and forth while assistant drivers provided directions and warnings in loud voices punctuated with emphatic gestures. We sat in the shade, near the railing on the balcony outside the second floor restaurant, drinking ice cold Cokes and eating the red peanuts and hard cheese we had brought from the health food store in Kabul.

I was sitting across from Patsy, a volunteer who had been briefly and casually involved with Chuck. Patsy's mother had come to Afghanistan to visit her—something which I found incomprehensible—and she had picked up an American highschool teacher somewhere along the way. So we sat there, the four of us, in the swirling smells of over-ripe fruit and vegetables, diesel fuel, and rotting meat mingled with the cool pungent promise of the slowly moving river, watching the near chaos below us. The temperature was in the nineties, at least, and the shade was wonderful. We had come here in a Mercedes bus with ruthlessly efficient air-conditioning and had been floored by the heat when we stepped out in the village.

We were on our way to Bamiyan. I had run into Patsy at the Peace Corps office where she introduced me to her mother. And

I had been invited to join them in this outing. Bob, the school-teacher, was part of the group by the time I met everyone at the bus stop this morning. He looked to be in his late forties or early fifties and was spending his summer wandering around this part of the world. His wandering eye had spotted Patsy's mother.

Bamiyan is a mountain valley about two hundred miles north-west of Kabul. The main highway had taken care of the bulk of the northern part of the journey and, when we left the village, we would begin the western leg. We had about a hundred miles to go, on a dirt road through the foothills of the Hindu Kush Mountains.

As we sat drinking our Cokes, a caravan came through town, heading west. It moved, it seemed, in its own silent realm with only the faint tinkling of bells reaching our table. It was a large caravan, perhaps sixty or seventy people, a few dozen camels, and a half dozen horses. The people walked alongside their animals, silently, with wonderful posture and brightly colored clothing.

Camels walk funny. They bend their knees as if they don't quite trust the surface and the front legs seem to move independently of the back legs. It was always hard to picture, but I think that un-like horses, which move their legs in a diagonal pattern (first right front and left rear moving, then left front and right rear), camels move the legs on the left, then the legs on the right, the whole process made workable by virtue of their pompous grace.

Outside of old cartoons, I've never seen a camel spit, but they look like animals that would really like to hock up a big loogie and let it fly. Camels stare at you with contempt, rolling their eyes while arching their necks and cocking their heads to one side. They aren't like horses, all nerves and muscles. Camels look as if they like to ponder things before doing anything radical like mov-ing or stopping, but they don't look particularly bright. The only sound they make comes across like a vague protest or reluctant agreement and could be confused with the grinding noise gener-ated when trying to shift gears in a bad transmission.

It is not possible, I think, for a person from the Western world to see a real camel caravan and not find it wonderful. Given the destruction of the roads in Afghanistan over the last twenty years, perhaps there will be a role for the camel caravans when all the foreigners finally leave.

———————

The bus broke down about forty or fifty minutes after leaving the village where we had seen the caravan. There was a really serious mechanical sound from the undercarriage, so the driver immediately killed the engine and coasted to the side of the road. The driver and his partner had a serious low-voiced discussion before getting out of the bus and looking underneath. The only sound was the ticking of the bus as it cooled and an occasional word or phrase from the drivers drifting in through the open doors. The drivers came back into the bus and told all of us to get out so that they could fix the problem.

Patsy, her mother, Bob and I were the only non-Afghans among the twenty-or-so passengers on the bus. Everyone spoke in low voices, as if in a church, as we stepped out of the bus into the dust of the road. I wandered back along the bus and then squatted to see what had happened. When I stood up, Bob was standing there.

"It's the universal joint," I told him.

"Really?"

"The driveshaft's lying in the dirt."

"What do you think they're going to do?"

"I have no idea," I said. "They told us they are going to fix it."

"Do you think they can?"

"Maybe it was just a loose bolt, vibrating free. That would be fixable, but if something actually broke . . ."

Bob and I looked at the white length of road stretching from one horizon to the other through the narrow arid valley. There was nothing to say. We were probably in the only vehicle passing through here today. At some point—probably tomorrow—another bus would come through. Maybe a truck.

Bob drifted off to talk with Patsy's mother and I walked from the dead white dirt of the road to the barely sentient, light-brown landscape. I didn't go too far from the road, but I wanted to be in the country itself, not on one of the narrow tracks used by tourists. It was silly, but at the time it felt like an important distinction. I grabbed a handful of hard dry soil and crumbled it in my hands as I turned to watch my fellow travelers.

Years later, I would be standing under Pennsylvania Station in Manhattan, waiting for my train back to Long Island. My train didn't arrive. The next train didn't arrive either and the platform was getting crowded. There were at least three trainloads of people standing in an area designed for one, and yet everyone was patient and quiet. We were all finished reading our newspapers and our paper cups of coffee with the Grecian scrolls were long empty. I had been standing there for about an hour when a voice shimmering with frustration rang out from farther down the platform: Where the hell is the goddamn train? There was a pause of almost a minute, then someone calmly said, loudly enough for all of us to hear, "He must be from New Jersey," and a thousand people burst out laughing.

That was the nearest experience to standing beside the road on the way to Bamiyan, my hands dirty from the soil and ears deafened by the silence. Patsy and her mother had walked down the road and were now heading back, leaning in as they talked. Bob was angled against the bus, legs braced in the dust of the road, reading a guidebook while the Afghan passengers meandered singly and in small groups in the vicinity of the bus. The driver and his partner worked in silence under the Mercedes, periodically exchanging brief observations.

The sky stretched pale blue over the dull landscape, trapping us under its bowl.

We were stopped for about an hour, maybe slightly less. Then the two men emerged from under the bus, wiping their hands on their now-filthy pants, and telling us we could get back into the bus.

"They didn't even curse," Bob said. "And the mechanic really smashed his finger . . . did you see it?"

"It's amazing," I agreed. "I can't imagine doing what they did without a few choice words."

Patsy said, "Yeah, but Americans would think that something had gone wrong, where here it's just inshallah."

That was it, of course. Inshallah. It was God's will in this God-saturated land that the bus would break down and their trust in God made it merely a test. They would fix the bus or they would not, inshallah, so there is no need to get angry. One cannot be angry with God. One cannot be angry at the very organization of life.

———————

Bamiyan was a stop on the southern silk road out of China, which was a major trade route by the second century. Goods from the Roman Empire made their way east while silk and other trade goods flowed west out of the Chinese Han Empire. This was not an easy trade route. The Hindu Kush Mountains are an extension of the Himalayas, which means they are not to be taken lightly as obstacles. And they are barren rocky piles of arid land that must have made small valleys like Bamiyan look like paradise.

It looked pretty damn good to me, too, after the rigorous ride in the Mercedes bus. The dust from the road had overwhelmed both the air-conditioning and my mucus membranes, so I had been inhaling dust straight into my lungs for almost an hour by the time the green trees of Bamiyan burst into view.

Two things dominated the Bamiyan Valley. The first was the luxurious vegetation growing on the banks of the stream. The green of the trees and of the irrigated cropland initially shocked, then soothed, eyes that had become adapted to a light-brown universe. The second thing was the cliff.

The cliff itself was impressive, looking almost like a dam holding back the churning flood of the Hindu Kush piled up behind it. But the cliffs were pierced with man-made openings that led to a warren of cave dwellings behind the cliff face. Our guide told us that originally the cliff face had been covered with scaffolding serving as vertical city "streets." It was also possible to move from cave to cave using internal connecting tunnels, although not all of the caves were linked. But even this cliff city was not the most impressive thing.

The most impressive sights in Bamiyan, and possibly some of the most impressive sights anywhere in the world, were the enormous sandstone Buddhas. The Large Buddha was one hundred seventy-five feet tall while the Small Buddha was a mere one hundred and twenty. Both Buddhas were deeply recessed into the sandstone cliff in what appeared to be perfectly symmetrical niches painted in brightly-colored patterns. The Small Buddha was believed to be the older of the two, created sometime in the third century A.D. The Large Buddha was created about two hundred years later. But, as Louis Dupree, Afghan scholar and Chuck's neighbor, said, "Possibly all these dates are wrong." According to Dupree, though, there is a general consensus that the statues were created between 300 and 700 A.D., which makes sense, given that this was the Buddhist period in Afghanistan.

When I saw the statues, the faces had been neatly removed, if neatly is a word that can be applied to such destruction. The faces above the lips had been cut off, I was told, because of the Islamic prohibition against the use of images. I thought, when I saw this, that removing the faces had been an act of respect. Rather than destroy the statues, someone decided to remove the essence of the offense, leaving the remainder. The statues were no less impressive for being faceless and removing the faces showed infinitely more respect for the beliefs and symbols of different people than did, for example, the British soldiers shooting off the nose of the Sphinx.

We wandered the caves with a local Afghan as a guide. He knew the area the way a small boy knows a local forest; he knew where all the neat stuff was and he didn't get lost, but he had no understanding and little respect for the world around him. At one point, I thought Bob the School Teacher was going to kill him. We were in the caves, in one of the deeper rooms, with a lantern providing light. The guide wanted to point out that there was a band around the ceiling; an intricate design made of ridges of what looked like mud. He wanted to show us his favorite parts of it, which he did by throwing small stones.

"Stop doing that," Bob told him.

"Knocko," I said to the guide. "Stop throwing the stones. Just point; we can see what you mean."

But he couldn't contain himself and he threw one more stone, bringing down a small patch of the design. I picked up the fragment as gently as I could but it turned to dust in my fingers. Bob reached out to grab the guide, but Patsy and I managed to keep them separate and to move everyone out of that chamber. Bob ranted about it on and off for the rest of the day.

The second day, we rented horses and rode out along the stream to look at old fortifications. My horse walked into the middle of the stream and I couldn't get him to leave until he had his fill of water. Patsy and I climbed to the top of a ridge, and looked at the defensive positions that had been used to control the area. Against whom? I wondered: was this the Buddhists against the Muslims? The Chinese against the Iranians? The Iranians against the Indians? It looked too new to my untrained eyes to have been built by Alexander's armies and too old to have been designed to keep the British out.

I felt better those two days in Bamiyan than I had felt for a long time. Perhaps better than I have felt since. Standing on the end of the ridge, next to a broken watchtower, all of history poured through me. This was a place where cultures had once flowed, where it was possible to buy Han silk or Egyptian cotton, using Roman coins. You could almost see the caravans entering the valley, and the camps set up along the riverside. We had long since given up on the horses, and I ran all the way back into the town where we were staying, much to Patsy's irritation.

"I am not going to keep running!" she shouted at my back. I waved goodbye to her over my shoulder, almost helplessly because I simply could not contain myself. I couldn't walk. I couldn't settle down.

On Monday March 12, 2001, the United Nations confirmed that the Taliban had destroyed the statues in Bamiyan.

Koichiro Matsuura, the Director General of UNESCO described the destruction of the statues as "a crime against culture." He said, "It is abominable to witness the cold and calculated destruction of cultural properties which were the heritage of the Afghan people, and, indeed, of the whole of humanity."

The Taliban, along with the Russians and everyone else carrying a weapon in Afghanistan, have committed untold horrors. The Taliban, a rancid collection of ignorant bigots, had as its stated goal the destruction of Afghan culture and individual freedom. We will probably never know how many people the Taliban killed, directly or indirectly, or how many people they humiliated, beat, bullied, and abused. Largely as a result of their single-minded religious fanaticism, egged along by outside meddlers, the entire infrastructure of the country has been reduced to rubble and a generation grown up without education or stability.

I know this. And, in the face of this human cost, the destruction of the Buddhas should pale in significance. But it doesn't for me because I stood on the ridge in Bamiyan with freedom coursing through me, looking over a valley culture created by the coming together of nations and peoples. The destruction of the Buddhas symbolizes all the other horrors, as if having finally exhausted their ability to hurt the population, the Taliban turned to blowing up inanimate objects. Perhaps trees were next on their list of things to destroy. Perhaps rocks weighing more than one Bedford first gear were an affront to God.

Afghanistan may well be the Accidental Nation, formed from the pressures and peoples around it. But that makes it, ironically, a very cosmopolitan place: a place with a history of freedom and a bloody history of fighting repression. The Buddhas in Bamiyan represented that: Come to this green valley and rest and talk with others under the watchful eyes of the Buddha.

The Buddhas were really something to see. One day, inshallah, I would like to go back to Bamiyan.

BOILING WATER

CHUCK, ED, AND I WERE SHARING A SERVANT. HE WORKED AT their house three days a week and at my place two days a week. For this, I paid half his salary.

"Half?" I asked Chuck. "Why not two fifths?"

Chuck acted surprised. "Actually," he said, "you're the one getting the deal here. It's unfair, but we weren't going to mention it."

This was going to be good. One of Chuck's favorite sayings was "If you had some ham, we could have ham and eggs, if I had some eggs." I knew he was going to create a cloud of confusion and use it to get his way. "Tell me, Chuck, how this is unfair to you guys?"

"Well, there's three of us sharing . . . " he started, and I burst out laughing. "No, no, listen," he went on, "there's three of us, and you get him for two days while Ed and I only get him for a day and a half."

You have to love a guy who can spin bullshit this fast. He had already won because he would stick to this analysis no matter what happened. I put up a token offense.

"But there are two houses," I said. "That's what matters. He's at your house most of the time, so you should pay most of his wages. And if I went out and got three roommates, would you have to pay more? Does that make sense to you?"

"Do you have three roommates? If you get three roommates, we'll have to rethink this." He refused to generalize.

We argued like this for five or ten minutes, mostly as a kind of sport, since he wasn't going to budge. And the man worked for Chuck, after all, while I was the one trying to introduce a new situation.

Peace Corps volunteers have a difficult time with the whole servant thing. Americans, in general, are uncomfortable with the idea of servants, but Peace Corps members have volunteered for "the Toughest Job You'll Ever Love," and servants really clashed with that image. But having someone working for you makes life easier in numerous ways. For example, I could bargain until I was blue in the face, but I could never get prices as low as an Afghan could get. If the absolute basement-level price for something for a foreigner was twenty afghani, then an Afghan could get it for ten or twelve. If the Afghan worked for me, he would then tell me it cost sixteen or seventeen afghani, simultaneously pocketing a small profit and saving me some money. If something went wrong and a repair man was needed, having an Afghan who was not so much on your side as invested in you for the long-term, was crucial. A servant could overcome linguistic barriers, if nothing else, translating my bad Farsi and miming behavior into a fluent request or explanation. And having a servant was like having a paid guide to a culture.

I was living in Bill's old apartment. Bill had finally managed to get to India, the only reason he had joined the Peace Corps in the first place, and then had quit as soon as he returned to Kabul. It was a great apartment, way bigger than I needed. It even had a small balcony on the street side. I was on the second floor. Tony and Danny lived upstairs, and were, as far as I knew, still without female companionship. Once, I locked myself out of my apartment and went upstairs and swung from their balcony to mine, where I removed a small window to get in. Tony had been quite impressed.

One of the things a servant needed to do was boil water for drinking and cooking. Water had to be boiled for twenty minutes to be considered safe. This was clearly stated in the Peace Corps Handbook. Not for fifteen minutes or nineteen minutes, but for a full twenty minutes. In training, we were told this about three hundred times. Twenty minutes was probably excessive, but it made a good rule. All the volunteers had timers so that the people who worked for us would know when twenty minutes were up.

Someone at Chuck's house strongly suspected that our servant was boiling the water for only five or ten minutes. The servant, it was thought, was turning on the timer as soon as the flame was lit under the big pot of water, rather than waiting for the water to boil, then turning on the timer. They asked me if I had noticed this at my house but, like them, I was usually gone when the servant was home. So we had a talk with the man. Chuck showed him the timer and how it worked. We all stressed how important it was. It became apparent that he thought we were irrational. It was as if we were saying, "And before you enter any room, you must make four clicking noises" or "You have to wash the dishes using a counter-clockwise motion." Like any sane person dealing with crazed people making outlandish requests, our servant would nod his head and say, "Yes, good, I understand," and then forget about all of our nonsense as soon as we were out of sight.

So we thought that it must be a language problem. We brought the Peace Corps translator to Chuck's house and we all stood around the stove, looking at the huge kettle used to boil water. The translator told the man that he had to boil the water so that we could drink it. We all looked at each other: what she said sounded just like what we had told him.

"It takes too much time," he said. "First I have to boil the water in the big pot and then I have to let it cool down before dumping it in the water container." (We all had large water containers with a spigot at the bottom.)

"But you have to boil it, otherwise they can't drink it."

"If they only drink it when it is hot, why do I have to let it get cool? Why don't they just drink tea?"

"You have to boil it so that they don't get sick."

"I do boil it."

"But not for twenty minutes."

"It's boiling, what difference does it make how long?"

We all looked at one another. He was really fighting us on this one. He looked as if he was tired of being told to do things that made no sense to him. And, of course, we didn't know why it had to be twenty minutes, except that the Peace Corps handbook said twenty minutes, and every book any of us had ever read on camping or living abroad always said twenty minutes. We assumed that tests had been conducted somewhere.

"Tell him," I said, "that there are small bugs in the water and we are not used to them. They make us sick to the stomach. It takes twenty minutes of boiling to kill all the bugs."

He looked into the pot of clear, steaming water. "There are no bugs."

"Really small ones," one of us said.

He looked again, mocking us with his careful inspection of the clear water, then shook his head. "I don't see them."

"They are too small to see," I said.

"Then how do you know they are there?"

My first reaction was that this man knew nothing of modern science. I asked if there was a microscope at the Peace Corps office, but no one knew.

"What are you going to do, teach him biology?" Chuck asked. "Give me a break."

Then one of us, I forget who, said, "We have to boil the water because the Bible tells us we have to."

The translator looked at us, and we all said, "Tell him that." Our servant was a Muslim; he understood the authority of religious texts.

The translator told him what we suggested, and they had a long discussion that I couldn't completely follow. Then our servant turned to us and said that from now on he would boil the water for twenty minutes. All this stuff about invisible bugs was obviously bullshit, but he could respect our religious beliefs, especially since they seemed so important to us.

Apparently, invisible gods who can damn you to hell were far more plausible than invisible bugs which could only make you sick enough to die.

THE BANK

Since the school where I was going to work was between semesters, the director found me a temporary job at a bank in downtown Kabul. I was to teach graduates of the local university the ins and outs of writing business letters.

"But I don't know anything about writing business letters," I told Marty.

"There's a book. How hard can it be?" he asked. "Writing letters is just writing." I must have looked skeptical because he repeated, "And there's a book."

"I am not crazy about the idea of working in a bank. If I wanted a job in a bank, I wouldn't have joined the Peace Corps."

"But you'll do it."

"Sure," I said. "Until the real job starts."

"Yes, until the other job starts."

As it turned out, I liked working at the bank. The bank took selected university graduates and put them through an extensive training course in international business. The students were very good and the other teachers were friendly and helpful. It was an impressive operation.

I even had an office. I shared it with three other men, but we had our own uncle. This guy was the Jeeves of Babas; a thin, elegant man who wore his white shirt buttoned to the neck under his gray sport coat. He had me figured out by the second day. He knew how and when I liked my tea. He brought me two cookies for the morning break and he would run out to buy me cigarettes every afternoon. He wore an astrakan hat, normally a sign of high status, but he wore it with such authority that no one could dare question its appropriateness.

My favorite part of the job, though, was lunch.

The bank had a cafeteria and all of us were expected to troop downstairs at noon. The first day I was there, I exited the serving line having no idea where I was supposed to sit. I spotted some of my students and asked if I could join them at their table. I had a thoroughly enjoyable time. The students asked me endless questions about America that I used as a basis for asking them questions about Afghanistan. We spoke in both English and Farsi, all of us wanting to practice our foreign language skills. When lunch was over, we shook hands all around and then I climbed back up to my office where my colleagues told me I should never, ever sit with the students again.

I was a teacher. I needed to sit with the teachers.

"Oh," I said. "I didn't know. I will sit with you tomorrow." But I couldn't get off the hook simply by pleading ignorance and promising never to do it again. They weren't going to let me off that easily.

They told me that I was not showing proper respect for the other teachers. That they were embarrassed in front of the students. That it wouldn't do to appear too friendly. This went on and on, each of the teachers in my office taking a turn telling me how the entire social structure would collapse if this sort of behavior became commonplace.

After the first day, I ate with the other teachers, a dull group of fastidious men who rarely talked and who almost succeeded in spoiling the pleasures of lunch at the bank.

I liked lunch at the bank. It made me feel like a local. We would all put down our pencils and our grade books, shrug into our sport coats, and tramp downstairs in an ever-growing Dickensian line, picking up threadbare bureaucrats as we walked up the hall and down the stairs. Sometimes I became aware of my place in the crowd of men walking to lunch and it would strike me as so absurd that I was here, one of them, on my way to a cafeteria of all places, that I would burst out laughing.

One joins the Peace Corps, after all, to seek adventure and to experience strange exotic situations. Back in Tashkurgan, I had sat in the dirt beside an irrigation ditch, planning how to divert the water into one of the compounds. The late summer sun had beaten down on us, turning the land golden while we sat huddled together arguing about various strategies. A week or so after that, I had gotten in a huge verbal fight with a man who was beating a horse that had been driven to its knees by the mud and the weight of its load. We had yelled at each other, faces inches apart, and I had torn the stick out of his hand as he raised it to beat the horse into obedience. I had unharnessed the horse, led it up the slippery, muddy slope and then told the Afghan that he and I would push the damn cart up to the road. That was the Peace Corps, so what was this?

This, I knew as I went down the stairs with all my fellow workers, was the most exotic thing I would do as a volunteer. Teaching is mostly an individual activity, unrelated to what other teachers are doing, and so normally collegiality is worn lightly. But here we were treated as office workers and I was expected to act as one of them and be treated like one of them. When I taught at the schools I would show up for my courses and leave when my courses were over. At the bank, I put in a routine six-hour day, and was expected to be in my office when I wasn't teaching a class.

Any tourist could stop a horse from being beaten, but none of them could wait in line at the cafeteria in the bank.

And then there was the lunch itself. There were no choices, but the meal changed from day to day. Each day, the meal consisted of an enormous heap of rice: as much rice as can be piled on a standard dinner plate by a professional Afghan rice-piler. It was a lot of rice. At the summit of the mountain of rice was a tablespoon of sauce. There were three sauces, but I only remember two of them: meat sauce and garbonzo bean sauce. Sauce may not be the right word. It was a tablespoon of thick, pasty stuff; like a stew left to simmer too long. The sauce was thick enough that it sat on top of the rice rather than running into it. The meat sauce had one bite-sized piece of beef, two if you were lucky. The garbonzo bean sauce would usually have three or four actual beans in it, but mostly consisted of beans mashed into a paste slightly more liquid than Mexican re-fried beans.

The trick, which took me a week to master, was to get some of the sauce in every bite and to completely clean the plate. The first day I ran out of sauce halfway through the stack of rice and had to eat the second half dry because it was unacceptable to leave half of your food on a plate. My favorite was the bean sauce. I wasn't there long enough to figure out the pattern, so each day was a surprise and I was always disappointed if the sauce was not garbonzo beans.

Garbonzo beans are the essence of no-taste. They are not taste-less, which implies a sort of sensory neutrality. Rather, garbonzo beans are a kind of negative taste. They take away, slightly, the flavor of other foods or of whatever taste you may have in your mouth. So it took a bit of culinary daring to couple garbonzo beans with steamed white rice. Less daring souls would have feared that the deficit created in this unnatural mating would have rendered the end result inedible given that, since two negatives equal a positive, taking nothing from nothing would equal something bad.

But instead you got a lunch of tremendous subtlety, in which a hefty spoonful of rice could be dipped ever so slightly into the congealing pool of sauce—sometimes only one or two grains actually making contact—and come away transformed.

And as we left the table to return to work, we would talk about the food.

"Lunch was good today," one of the other teachers would say.

"It was garbonzo bean sauce, my favorite."

"Everyone knows that, Mr. John."

BEING MEAN TO STUDENTS, PART TWO

IT WAS BABA AGAIN, KNOCKING AT MY DOOR.

"The director wants to see you, Mr. John."

The director. I had seen the director when I came on board at this school, but not since. "Does he want to see me now or after class?"

"I think now, Mr. John."

I was teaching English at the Telecommunications School outside of Kabul. The students were in their late teens and early twenties, giving the place the feel of a good community college. They were smart, these students, and focused. They spent most of their time in technology courses, learning how to set up, use, and repair telecommunications equipment. I taught them English, so they could read technical manuals, I suppose. I had them reading Jack London because he wrote in clear, simple prose and because he was the one writer all of the students had heard about. I typed pages of London's novels, fitting in definitions and synonyms in parentheses occasionally, and mimeographed them. We read them out loud in class.

One day a student read a passage that stunned the class into embarrassed silence. In the story, a man and woman were having a conversation. In the course of that conversation, the woman stood looking out the window and, after a while, the man went over to stand next to her. The student's voice faltered, then failed as he tried to read the sentence. There were a few titters from other students, but almost all of them were looking at their desks. Many were blushing.

"What?" I asked them. "The man and the woman are talking. Is there something about the conversation that you find confusing?"

They shook their heads. I read the sentence a few times to myself: man and woman talking, woman at window, man goes to window, man and woman continue talking. What was the problem here? Were they so disturbed by the fact that a man and woman were talking? Was it the tone of the conversation? The implied equality of it? What was going on?

I read the passage out loud and some of the students laughed. There was something in this passage which was clear to the students and I was missing it altogether. Looking at them, I started to laugh too. "What is it?" I asked them. "What is so funny?"

All of the students stared at me, afraid to say anything. I sat on the edge of my table. "For Americans," I said, "this is not a funny story. Tell me why it is funny for you. Please."

A minute passed. One student raised his hand and I called on him.

"They are talking and they are having sex right in front of the window," he told me.

I started to laugh and all of the students joined in now. I had no idea what they were talking about. When the laughter died down, I asked them why they thought the two people were having sex. Again, the students were reluctant to talk, so I pointed at the student who told me they were having sex and asked him how he knew.

"It says, so, Mr. John," he told me. "It says 'he joined her at the window.'"

The students roared with laughter when he finished actually saying the words and, after a second or two, so did I. These were technology students, learning technical terms, and they thought of join only in its mechanical sense. Before coming to my class, they had spent hours joining together wires, pieces of equipment, and structural elements.

I told the student who had dared to talk to go stand by the window. "Now," I said, "I am going to join you there." The rest of the class went out of control, hooting and yelling. I walked over and stood beside him, looking out the window. "See? I've joined you at the window."

I spent the next ten minutes having various students joining each other at the window. I loved teaching English.

But today I had to see the director, so I told the class to be quiet, that I would be back in ten minutes.

The director sat behind his desk and Uncle went to stand beside him. The director was looking at my roll books. The roll books looked like the ones used in U.S. schools: large spiral notebooks with columns for all the days in the semester and rows for all of the students. He ponderously flipped the long pages, dramatically shaking his head in dismay and disbelief. He looked up at me. "You have changed these documents."

"Changed them in what sense?" We were speaking in English.

"You have changed them. See? Here, and here. Here, too." His thick finger stabbed at the offending spots. I looked closely. The penciled marks had been erased and changed.

"Oh," I said. "That isn't anything. I marked the students absent and then the students came in late. So I corrected the roll."

"Corrected," he said, as if the word had no place in our discussion. "You changed the roll sheet."

I nodded. "Yes. I changed it because I had indicated the student wasn't in class, then the student came into the class. I wanted the roll to be accurate."

"The roll book," he said, "is a government document."

"Yes," I agreed. "So it needs to be accurate."

"No," he replied. "So it cannot be changed."

"Oh." I thought about this for a few seconds. "So I should take roll a few minutes into the class so that this doesn't happen again."

He shook his head, wondering how he had gotten saddled with this American who seemed incapable of understanding the simplest things. "No, you must take roll as soon as the bell rings. That is the law."

"What about the students who have to come all the way in from the lab course?" I asked. "It's a long way and they are often a few minutes late."

"Being late is being absent."

"Oh." I thought about this. There were five or six students who were routinely late in each class I taught. They were good students, like most of the students here. "But the students are not allowed to miss class."

"That is the point," he told me. "Any student who misses three classes will be expelled."

"Expelled."

"That is the rule," he told me. "You should go back to your class now."

I took the roll book with me and went back to my classroom. I got the students settled down and told them I had something very serious to tell them.

"The director explained to me that this is a government document," I said, holding up the roll book. "I did not know this. Sometimes when you came in late, I would change the mark in the book from absent to present. The director told me that this could get the school into a lot of trouble. Does everyone understand what I'm saying?" I let them talk to each other in Farsi until they all nodded their heads that they understood.

"From now on," I said, "I will not change the roll book. If you are late, then I will mark you absent."

"But Mr. John, it takes too long to get here from the lab class."

"You will have to run. I can't change the grade book and I must take roll when the bell rings. Is this clear? If you have to go to the bathroom, come to class first, then ask to go to the bathroom."

The room was dead silent as they thought about this.

"And this is very important. Some of you already have two absences. If you are absent one more time, you will not be allowed to stay in this school. I will read the names of all the students with two absences."

I read the names into the gloom I had created, then started the most subdued class session I had ever taught.

Inevitably, the next day rolled around and I went to class with the heart of a hangman.

The bell rang. I looked for a pencil, which took a bit of time. I finally found one, but its point was less than adequate for an official government document, so I spent a good minute or so sharpening it. Then I sat on the edge of my table and began reading the roll. It was the eighth person, I think, who didn't answer. I left the space blank and continued reading. Another late student. Then another. I got to the end of the roster and, without pausing, read the first of the missed names.

"Present."

I looked up and saw him sitting in his seat. Thank God. I called the next name. No answer. I called the last of the missed names.

"Present."

I read the name of the second missing student. No answer. I marked him absent and put the book away. The student who was missing had two previous absences.

We were barely into our warm-up drills when the missing student burst, Kramer-like, into the classroom. All the students looked at him, then at me.

"Don't sit down," I told him. "Go see the director."

"Let me stay. It wasn't my fault."

I was furious at him. Anger washed through me, instantly overwhelming me. He had behaved so carelessly and now I was forced to kick him out of my class and out of the school.

"I told you!" I yelled at him. "I told you that you had to be here on time. That I had to mark you absent if you were late. I told you!" I wanted to hit him. I wanted to console him. "Now, stop talking and get out of here! Go to the director's office."

I could feel my muscles shaking and my heart pounding. My face must have been bright red. The other students made themselves invisible while I stared at the late student, standing by the door. I watched his face collapse as all hope left it, as he realized that neither charm nor excuses would allow him to put his books on the desk, to sit down and remain part of the course. I turned and walked to the window where I put my hands on the sill, looking out but seeing nothing. I heard the door close behind me and I closed my eyes.

He would be asked to leave today. Uncle would walk him from the director's office to the dorm and all his possessions would be shoveled into a sack or a bundle. He would be marched to the gate and told not to come back. The former student would have to find a way back to his village, where he had once been their shining star, their brightest hope, and tell them that he had failed. He had to explain to his family, his neighbors, and to the local leaders that he was not going to be a government technician or official, working in the modern area of telecommunications with a chance, perhaps, to visit the Soviet Union or East Germany. He had failed. I could almost see him, standing in the dust outside the gate, near the road, wondering what he was going to do, wondering where he was going to go.

I turned back to the class and continued drilling the difference between the pee sound and the eff sound. Afghans couldn't hear the difference between "I write with a pen" and "I write with a fen."

Normally, this was a fun exercise.

THE LAST DAYS

THE GAMES

I was about halfway to Chicken Street when I saw the men playing the rock game. I had seen men playing this before, but I could never figure out the rules. Two or three men squatted down and used their fingers or a stick to draw a geometric pattern in the dirt. All the players picked up small pebbles and used them as markers.

It was a beautiful day—in that slow, lazy way that Afghan days can be beautiful—and it was Saturday, so I had no particular place to go. I squatted next to the players, watching them draw the pattern in the dirt and collect small stones.

"*Salaam a'laikim,*" one man said to me.

"*A'laikim a salaam,*" I responded. "How are you? Are you good?"

"How are you? Are you good?"

"I'm good. Would you like a cigarette?" I passed out cigarettes to the four men. Three of them carefully put the cigarettes in their pockets. I lit mine and held my match out for the fourth man. He got his cigarette going and then went back looking for small stones, the smell of tobacco smoke sharp in the cool morning air. There was a scrawny tree in the small patch of dirt between the sidewalk and the street, and the fluttering of the leaves in the soft morning breeze threw dancing shadows over the game surface.

"Do you want to play?"

"Oh, no. I don't understand this game. I want to see how you play."

So I watched the two men play, their friends leaning over and offering advice. I would ask questions about the moves they were making and they would stop and explain them to me. It was a version of what we called, when I was growing up, Chinese Checkers. Chinese Checkers, like checkers, is one of those games that is simple in concept, but almost infinite in the ways any particular game can unfold.

Once I saw how it was played, I paid less attention and gradually drifted into a pleasant stupor, the morning washing quietly over me. The sun was already warm but not unpleasant, and it felt good against the faint chill in the air. And it also felt good to be squatting next to these men, letting the time pass by aimlessly, tangled up in the activity swirling around us. The first game ended with the smoker losing and then, with lots of post-game analysis, a second game was set up. A boy was sent to get us some tea.

I heard a camera go off. I looked up, squinting into the sunlight, and saw a European man with a camera.

"Hey," I said. I sipped my tea.

"Hello. What are these men doing?"

"Playing a game. It's like Chinese Checkers."

"I don't know that game," he said, and took another picture. An Englishman, by the sound of him.

I explained it to him, pointing out the goals and strategies. "It's the same basic idea as checkers, but the board isn't square."

He took another picture and I asked him to stop. This wasn't a zoo. He put the lens cap back on and then leaned in to watch. He wanted to talk, not understanding how quiet the country was, so I gave short answers, then no answers, and he settled into the rhythm of the day.

The smoker was getting badly beaten in the second game, needing more and more time to think about fewer and fewer options. His friends were teasing him.

Ed walked up. "Are you going to the game?" he asked me.

"Yeah. It's not for another hour or so, right?"

"Hour and a half. They playing the rock game?"

"Yeah. Chuck going?"

"As far as I know," he said. "Looks like checkers, kind of."

"Basically. Where are you going now?"

"Tritoni's," he said.

"That's where I was going, then I sort of got stuck here."

We said goodbye, saying we'd meet later. Actually, I would have to head home first, to change my shoes, so I was running out of time, especially if I wanted to get something to eat.

"What game was he talking about?" the Englishman asked me.

"Who?"

"Your friend. He asked if you were going to the game."

"Oh, it's a softball game. We're playing the Marines today."

He looked disappointed. "I thought you might be going to some sort of ethnic game."

I acted confused. "I am," I told him. "It's an American ethnic game. It's full of rituals and funny costumes. We say things like 'batta batta batta' and 'atta boy' and we all add the ee sound to our names: Johnny, Bobby, Eddy. It's an ethnic game."

"I mean I thought it was an Afghan game."

"Nope."

I said long good-byes to the men playing the rock game and then stood up. I said goodbye to the Englishman.

I think that was the last softball game before the coup.

THE COUP

I WAS A LITTLE EARLY, SO I WAS DAWDLING ALONG, RIDING THE bicycle with no hands, making my way down the deserted street in long sweeping arcs. I forget who we were scheduled to play softball against that day, perhaps the Brits, but as it turned out, it really didn't matter. It was one of those late spring mornings where you could feel the heat building over the horizon, just starting to creep over the rocky piles surrounding the city, but I was riding through the last of the night-cooled air and it felt like all was right with the world.

I didn't remember him at first, when he ran out into the street, waving his arms. He was in his early twenties, with short hair, wearing sports clothes. He looked like Kansas to me, wheat fields and blue-eyed girlfriends.

"Hey," he yelled. "Stop!"

Then I knew who he was. He was one of the Marines. I recognized him from a ball game we played a week or two ago. I remember looking at the building he had run out of and thinking, so this is where the Marines live.

"Where are you going?" he asked. He was leaning forward, on the balls of his feet.

"To the softball game," I said. "Why? What's up?"

He looked around, so I looked around, too. It was a broad, empty street. Nothing moved. I didn't hear anything at all.

"Is there a war?" he asked me.

"What? A war?" And then we both looked around again. No war in sight.

"Yeah," he said. "I was running past the radio station and there were tanks all around it."

"Really?" I had very little to offer in this conversation. "Were they firing at the station?"

He nodded, then shook his head. "Yeah, tanks and soldiers, but they weren't firing at anything."

"Have you been back to your barracks, or your home, whatever?" I asked. "If there's a war, the Embassy will let you guys know first."

"Yeah, right. Right. I was just going back in when I saw you and thought you might know something. I'd better get back and talk to the sergeant." He nodded a few times, then spun and ran about ten feet. He turned to look at me. "Where will you go?"

I had no idea. "I think I'll just head out to the field and see if anyone there knows what's going on."

"Yeah," he said, then turned again, and ran toward his house.

Before I got to the field, I ran into Charlie McCarthy. I forget his real name. He was a big, good-looking guy from Colorado or Utah—someplace, at any rate, with lots of snow, because I remember he told us he was on the ski patrol. I called him Charlie McCarthy because his girlfriend came to visit him in Afghanistan and he wouldn't let her speak to us. Whenever anyone asked her a question, he would answer for her.

"So, Cathy, how do you like Kabul?"

"She liked Chicken Street, but the meat bazaar was a little much for her."

"Oh, well, have you been out of the city, Cathy?"

"She's nervous about leaving Kabul, but I'm thinking of taking her to Ghazni next weekend."

And she would just sit there, a pretty woman with a nice smile on her face and eyes watching everyone. Chuck and Ed began answering for each other when they were around Charley and Cathy, but Charley never noticed that they were mocking him.

Charley, too, was riding out to the softball field and we met when he cut in from a side street, riding at full speed as he always did. I waved him to a stop and pulled up beside him.

"I ran into one of the Marines," I told him, "and he said he thought there was a revolution or something. He said the radio station was surrounded by tanks."

"I heard some explosions earlier this morning," he said. "I didn't know what they were."

We talked for a while, speculating on things beyond our ken, then decided to head over to Kay's house. Kay was the unofficial center of the Peace Corps in Afghanistan. No one that I knew would think about going over to the director's house or to Marty's house. First, we would rely on each other, then if things were getting out of hand, we'd go talk with Kay. The first time I went to the director's house was the day I decided to leave Afghanistan. And Kay's husband was one of the Embassy guys, which meant that she would probably know what was going on.

By the time we got to Kay's house, we could hear the sporadic rattle of small arms fire coming from various parts of the city. Periodically, there would be the thud of an explosion as heavier weapons were brought into play. Looking down the side streets as we pedaled past, we could see military vehicles on the move and, occasionally, squads of soldiers on foot. Chuck was standing behind Kay when she opened the door.

There must have been ten or a dozen of us there by midday. If we had been in the States, we would have turned on the radio or the television to get some information. But we were in Afghanistan, so we did what people always do when confronted with high levels of uncertainty and low levels of information: we speculated.

Chuck decided he was in charge. He found Kay's husband's stock of weapons—a small revolver, a shotgun, and a hunting rifle—and passed them out. He gave Kay the revolver, me the shotgun, and kept the rifle for himself. He had made me his lieutenant. He and I, he said, were the only ones with military experience and so we were going to establish defenses against the inevitable attack.

I asked Kay what Larry used the shotgun for and she told me it was for shooting birds. I jacked a shell out of the breech and looked at it. Deer slugs may have been helpful, but birdshot was really going to piss some people off—people who had much better weapons than we did. And, of course, many more people than we had. And all those damn tanks, not to mention the airplanes with the bombs sitting just outside the city.

It was my view that we should unload all the weapons and put them away. In the unlikely event that the soldiers did come, we should rely on Kay's diplomatic status. Fighting the Soviet-equipped military with weapons designed to kill rodents struck me as unwise.

Chuck disagreed. He was in command mode, which I must admit was quite impressive. I could see him organizing the Ala-mo until there was no one left to organize, or rallying the Brit-ish troops retreating from the Zulu tribesmen. It bothered me, of course, that these images were of staggering military failures. Chuck went upstairs to check fields of fire and I unloaded the shotgun and leaned it in a corner.

And not surprisingly the soldiers never came, since there were no military objectives in Kay's neighborhood and, as a result, we never determined which would have been the better strategy. At that point, in the very beginning of Afghanistan's long col-lapse, it was simply that some elements of the Soviet-trained and equipped army were fighting other elements of the Soviet-trained and equipped army. It was a coup, which meant there was an army focused on a few clear objectives, rather than a bunch of rag-tag militia driven half-mad by ideological zeal, colossal igno-rance, and horrendous living conditions. If the Taliban had come into town, I would have been helping Chuck sharpen the steak knives and considering the weapons value of the barbecue tongs. But at that time in Afghanistan only the military was armed in any serious way and the military was very much a Westernized institution. Militarism is its own ideology and religion.

Waiting through the day for the Afghan army to attack Chuck became boring. We were in a house surrounded by a high wall.

We could see little and hear less. Our conversation had long run out of gas. It was late afternoon, so I decided to head home, thinking that once it got dark I would be unable to cross the city. It was Kay, I think, who suggested that I check on a Peace Corps couple who lived nearby.

They had a really nice house about three blocks from Kay's. New Afghan houses are similar to new houses in Mexico in that the clean simple lines feel both very traditional and extremely modern. Like everyone else in this neighborhood, this couple had not been directly involved in the day's events. I only knew them in passing—from Peace Corps events and from the softball games—but it was nice seeing them.

I told them that a lot of people were at Kay's house and that she had invited them to come over and join the group. They declined and we talked for a few minutes. They offered me a beer and we settled in just as the first bomb dropped.

"What the hell was that?"

"I saw some jets on the way over here. They must be dropping bombs downtown."

"I guess we should go down to the basement."

"Good idea."

We went down to the basement and stood drinking our beer and listening to the explosions.

"I can't stand this," the woman said after a few minutes. We could feel the dull, dense sound of the explosions.

"You mean, being in the basement?" I asked and she nodded.

"Oh, God, me neither," her husband said. "I didn't want to say anything. Let's go upstairs. We can look out the window."

It was very early evening by now and as we watched we began to lose the planes in the fading light. They were Soviet MiGs with an old-fashioned look about them. Later, an Afghan would tell me that the pilots were Soviets, because Afghans were incapable of flying well enough to be effective. We could see them when they circled high above the city, but then they would dive at a steep angle and fire rockets at the government center. When they were low with the mountains as a backdrop, I would lose them until the failing sun caught them in their sharp climbs after their attack runs. We drank our beer and watched. Once, a plane fired too early and we watched the rocket smash into the houses piled high in their poverty on the hill across the city.

We had a second beer and watched until it was too dark to see anything except the bright flashes of the explosions, which looked delicate and festive, and relatively harmless. It reminded me of a night in Vietnam when I had been running for shelter during a rocket attack and then stopped to watch when the ammo dump was hit and all the ordinance started to go off like the Fourth of July at Disneyland. The air attack on Kabul was both pretty and terrible, but while the pretty was obvious, we had to keep reminding ourselves that it was also terrible. We caught ourselves ooohing once or twice at the splashes of light and then, embarrassed, we decided to go back downstairs.

"Do you want to stay here tonight?"

"No, I think I'll go home."

"Are you sure you'll be safe?"

"I'll cut across the hill," I told them. "If it looks dangerous, I'll come back."

Kabul wraps around a low, rounded hill. The hill was undeveloped, used primarily by nomad caravans as a camp site. Kay lived close to one side of the hill and my neighborhood was a block or two from the hill, about a third of the way around. It was only a few blocks to the base of the hill where I found a faint path, made even fainter by the darkness, leading in the general direction of my apartment. This was all theoretical, this shortcut. I wanted to avoid the streets—rounding a corner in the dark and running into a military patrol struck me as a sure way to cut short my stay in Afghanistan—but although I had thought about this route before, I had never had any real motivation for trying it out.

I was walking slowly because I was on a dirt path in the dark. The hillside would flash into faint perspective whenever there was a particularly large explosion across town; light up, then get momentarily darker so quickly that I had to recall the landscape rather than look at it. It was like being guided by memories. During one such moment I saw the shapes of people moving on the hillside, and stopped walking.

I could hear the jets flying over the city and the sounds of the battle taking place, but there were no sounds on the hillside. No. Not quite no sounds, I realized as I stood there. There were faint sounds: people quietly shifting positions to get more comfortable, someone walking a few paces, an occasional softly-voiced remark. What was missing was the inevitable clank of equipment, the scuffle of a hard-soled combat boot, or the harsh sounds of hostile intent hissing out in whispered orders and furtive movements. So, not soldiers.

Nomads, I thought.

It is difficult to get more romantic than an Afghan nomad. Perhaps the American Plains Indians, mounted on horses and following the buffalo, or Cossacks sweeping over a hill on their ponies, would have a comparable romantic image. But Indians have never really done it for me—too much, perhaps, of that Mr. Coyote talking to Mr. Chicken stuff—and I knew very little about life on the Russian Steppes. Ever since the trip to Bamiyan, though, I had been in love with the nomads. I turned my head very slowly, looking for the yurts, and found them a dozen yards or so up the hill and about two or three dozen yards in front of me. Two yurts, maybe three: a small group.

I walked slowly and kept my arms and hands well away from my body, so that my silhouette would indicate an unarmed man. I wasn't too worried about being confused for a soldier because soldiers don't walk the way I was walking; loose and free, unarmored, unarmed, without supplies or ill-fitting clothing. I walked slowly now because it was still dark and because a moment ago the hill had been an empty place that I needed to traverse, and now it was a camp and I felt like a trespasser, that I needed to ask permission to pass.

A man approached me. I could barely make him out. Tall, wrapped in dark clothing. I stopped and he stood less than two feet away from me, which is close, an almost intimate distance for complete strangers, but we were standing in the dark, on a hillside, watching a war across the valley, and it seemed like exactly the right distance for the situation. I said hello, quietly, speaking as formally as I knew how. We went through the normal conversational rituals and then turned and faced the city. There were two explosions in quick succession, some rifle fire, then a lull.

"They're crazy down there," I said.

"I don't know what they are doing," he said.

It was already getting cool and I was still dressed for playing softball in the midday heat. Standing on a hillside with a nomad leader, watching people killing each other over inconsequential differences, created an odd tension for me. On the one hand, I was willing to be adopted into this man's group, to be offered his dark-eyed daughter and, perhaps, a camel. A camel and a yurt, and a lifetime spent walking in the dust and the silence of the Afghan back-country.

On the other hand, I knew I was closer to the people down below, the people doing the killing and the dying. I was part of the world that created the weapons that were lighting up the night sky. I had been in the military and had once clanked around a small country, armed and armored, wearing odd, ill-fitting clothes. The battle across town was, at this point, without any known purpose—it would be weeks before the new government identified itself as Communist—but it had the feel of global politics, of international realignments. That was the world I knew. I pictured Afghanistan as the bright green area on the globe, south of the Soviet Union, east of Iran, west of the subcontinent.

If the man I was standing with gave me his daughter's hand, a camel, and a yurt, I would join him in wandering the country, but I would always know that now we were getting closer to the light blue area where the Ayatollah ruled and hated all things American, or to the yellow country where the Communists lived who have vowed to bury the capitalists.

We stood there for a long time, rarely speaking. A few people settled around us. They sat on their haunches, watching the cryptic streams and flashes of light; messages encoded by the distance until they became meaningless to us. I gave the man a cigarette that he didn't smoke, and he told me he didn't have any tea to offer. No fires, he said. Then I told him goodnight and wished him well. I walked through his camp and around the hill to my neighborhood.

I arrived home without incident. I read for an hour or so, then went to sleep.

WHAT DIFFERENCE DOES IT MAKE?

"WHAT DON'T YOU UNDERSTAND, MR. JOHN?"

He looked so earnest, sitting there in the front row of the classroom. This was our first day back after the coup, and everyone was a little nervous. There was a tank right outside the building. You could see it from the windows if you looked to the left through the trees. The tank would start up periodically, bellowing smoke and clanking like an arthritic dinosaur as it moved about in the small clearing, apparently trying to get comfortable before once again falling quiet and dozing in the midday sun, soldiers scattered about it like so many pebbles.

"I don't understand how these things happen," I said. "The army is made up of draftees who are assigned to various units . . . that's how it works, isn't it? Or are you kept in the same unit if you're all from the same village?"

"No," another student answered, "you don't get to stay with the people from your village."

"You can be sent anywhere," another added. The only thing keeping these men out of the draft was being enrolled in this school. It wasn't clear how long that would last.

"This is what I don't understand," I said. "If you happen to be in a unit that supports the government, then you fight for the government. But if you happen to be in a unit that supports the coup, then you fight against the government. It's just a matter of chance."

They all nodded. That was how it worked.

"But what if you like the government and are in a unit that is fighting against it?"

"You have to do what the members of your unit do." They seemed confused by my failure to understand how coups worked.

"But you could end up shooting people from your own village. People you grew up with."

They nodded and looked glum. Yes, indeed, that could very well happen.

"So you are shooting people you like in order to help people you don't like."

There was a long pause. They looked at one another, unsure what to say to me. Finally a boy in the back raised his hand and I called on him.

"What don't you understand?" he asked me.

I shook my head at the size of the gap between us. "I guess I don't understand why you would shoot people you liked to help people you didn't like."

He was maybe nineteen, this young man, with eyes that seemed at that moment to be infinitely old. He started speaking hesitantly, as if he may have misunderstood my point. "Once you start killing people, Mr. John," he said, "what difference does it make who they are?"

I was shocked. "It doesn't make any difference?"

"I don't think so."

I looked at the rest of the students. They were nodding their heads in agreement. We had stumbled into a moral divide. Standing in the classroom, I found their attitude almost incomprehensible, but thinking about it later—and ever since—I think the students had a moral sense both stronger and more brittle than mine. It was stronger because they were completely baffled by my apparent willingness to divide people into those who were shootable and those who were not. Their rule was hard and fast: All people are morally equal, so you shouldn't shoot any of them. But this makes for a very brittle rule that, once violated, shatters into meaninglessness.

The Western tradition has few, if any rules that are quite so rigid. We have a basic rule: Don't kill anyone. But if you violate that, we have an infinite number of fallback positions. Was it in self-defense? Were you fighting evil? Did you kill in a just cause? Were you coerced? Were you, like, really, really angry? Had you recently eaten a lot of sugar? We have a moral system that resembles one of those Russian nesting dolls: each time you discard a moral rule, there's another rule right beneath it that looks almost the same, but is slightly smaller in scope.

I am sure that most of the young men who were in my class have been killed in the fighting over the last twenty years. That was the second to the last day I ever spoke with those students and I can still picture them, teetering on the edge of chaos, with only one rule as a safety line.

The next day, the soldiers came to the school.

NOT ARRESTED

FOR ME PERSONALLY, THE MOST IMMEDIATE IMPACT OF THE coup d'etat was that my bicycle was stolen and I had to take the bus to work. Riding a bicycle in a country where it is a major form of transportation was a huge amount of fun. I loved hauling ass down the main roads, the little bell on the handle bars jangling, weaving in and out of the four-wheeled, two-wheeled, two-footed traffic. But now I was back on public transportation and, as fate would have it, I missed the return bus after my classes were finished and had about an hour to kill.

The telecommunications school where I taught was located just out of town, on the main highway heading south toward the *East* Kabul Gorge. Just south of the school was the country's major telecommunications installation, which had been guarded by a tank since last week's coup. Across the street was a small roadside bazaar, a motorist's last chance for tea, food, and snacks before hitting the Gorge. With over an hour to kill, I decided to walk over to the bazaar, buy some cigarettes, then while away the time in a *chai hana*—a tea house. *Khana*

The guys on the tank looked at me curiously as I walked past on the other side of the road. I gave them a little wave and then ignored them. Staring at them seemed like a bad idea. I bought five cigarettes, which itself helped pass some time. Cigarettes always cost two afghanis apiece.

"Hello," I said to the shopkeeper. "How are you?"

"Hello. I am fine. How are you?"

"I am also fine. Are you good?"   *Well*

"Yes, I am good."   *Well*

"That is good. How much do you ask for one American cigarette?"

"One American cigarette? Do you mean this one?" He held up a pack of Winston Lights.

"I haven't decided yet. How much do you ask for one cigarette?"

"American?"

"Yes."

He thought about this for a minute, as if no one had ever asked such a question before and he had to calculate their cost for the first time.

"I think three afghanis."

"Three afghanis!" I said, shocked beyond belief that the value of a cigarette could be so miscalculated. The mistake was so large, the shopkeeper must have misunderstood what I wanted. There was, of course, no question of avarice, because everything was done in good faith. "I am sorry. I mean what is the cost of one American cigarette?"

"That is three afghanis."

I acted confused. "I buy cigarettes all over Afghanistan," I told him, "and I always pay only one afghani for an American cigarette."

He smiled. "Then you must mean this cigarette," he said and held up a pack of K2s, a Pakistani cigarette.

"No," I said, shaking my head, perplexed. One of us was very confused. "I buy American cigarettes or English cigarettes."

"English cigarettes?" He asked, sounding relieved, as if we had resolved the riddle. He held up a pack of Dunhills. "Like this?"

"Yes," I said. "How much do you ask for one of those?" I thought this was a very clever shopkeeper who realized I was not a tourist and so switched to English cigarettes so that he could change the price without any loss of face. A very sophisticated approach.

"Three afghanis," he said. Not so sophisticated after all.

"This is very expensive. I would like five English cigarettes for ten afghanis."

"English cigarettes?"

"Yes. For ten afghanis."

"Ten? Oh, that is impossible. I think twelve."

"But they are only worth five. I am already giving you too much."

"Ten, you said?"

"Yes. Ten."

"Good," he said, and we exchanged money for cigarettes. "Anything else?"

"No, thank you. Goodbye."

"Goodbye. Have a long life."

"Don't be tired."

Tea, for some reason, is standardized and so there is no haggling. I walked over to the tea house, sat on the *char poi* chair at the rickety table, ordered a pot of black tea, and lit a cigarette. This is how time is passed in Afghanistan.

On the walk back to the school to catch the bus, one of the soldiers waved. I waved back and continued walking. He became more emphatic and I realized he wanted me to cross the road and speak with him. He's bored, I thought. He'll ask me for a cigarette or for the time of day: Are you an American? Do you work at the school?

"Hello," I said, after I had crossed the road. "How are you?"

"What are you doing here?" he asked without any prelude.

This, you must understand, is very rude. An Afghan will tell you how he is doing and ask how you are at least twice, if not three times. This did not look good. I acted as if the conversation had not taken an unusual turn. I told him, in a cheerful voice, that I was an American Peace Corps volunteer and that I taught in the school. I pointed at the school, in case that needed clarification. Another man came up to me, an officer.

"You are a liar," he said.

This was really going downhill.

"No, I am not," I insisted. "Go over there. Ask them. They will tell you that I am a teacher from the Peace Corps."

"You are a spy!" he yelled. "You were seen dropping these photographs in the bazaar!" He waved a film strip with photographs of the King of Afghanistan, who had been deposed in the early seventies. It looked to me like the same picture that was on much of the currency I used on a daily basis.

I shook my head emphatically. I was getting a little angry. "You are mistaken. You go to the school and ask them who I am."

"I am going to go to the school. You sit here!" He pointed to a bench, then had a hurried conversation with two of the soldiers. They stayed behind with me; the rest went with the officer to the school.

I sat on a wooden bench in a small grove of trees. I was facing the road and one soldier sat on either side of me. The soldier on my left had a rifle. If my understanding of the Afghan army was accurate, the one on my right had the bullets. After about ten minutes, the U.S. Embassy car drove past, heading south. That was interesting, I thought. It's too late in the day to start driving to southern Afghanistan and there's nothing immediately south of here except the military base. I had the impression that Embassy staff always took the Land Rover on trips out of the city, rather than the sedan. The car would be turning around somewhere before the Gorge, I thought, and heading back. I figured another ten minutes or so.

I waited five minutes, then said to the soldiers, "I need to stand up, but I won't go anywhere."

"Good, but stay close."

"I will." I stood up and made a big production of stretching my back and legs. In a visual dictionary, my behavior could have illustrated both "stretching" and "bad acting." Big yawn, then I walked over to the nearest tree. Looked at the bark very closely, as if I had noticed something, then shook my head: nope, just a tree, as I had suspected. I was now ten feet closer to the road. I knelt to tie one shoe. I stood up, then knelt to tie the other. I was another two feet closer to the road. Time to reassure the guards, who were still sitting. I turned to them and said it was a nice day. They just looked at me. They didn't seem worried. It wasn't clear whether they thought in terms of days that were nice and days that weren't.

I wandered around, moving back and forth parallel to the road, which was about twenty feet away from me. I didn't want to seem to be moving away from them, but I wanted them to get used to me moving all the time. The rifle was held in the soldier's left hand, butt on the bench, his hand gripping the fore stock, well above the trigger. I heard a car in the distance, cutting through the still silence of the afternoon.

If it was the Embassy car, I would run out in the road, waving my arms. That was my plan. I was obviously a Westerner, if not obviously an American, and they would probably stop. I knew a lot of the Embassy staff by sight and I assumed they knew me the same way. Even if they didn't stop, perhaps someone would say, "Wasn't that Sumser talking with those soldiers? I wonder what he's up to?" There was another tree, closer to the road and I wandered over to it, and the soldiers stood up.

"Where are you going?"

I turned to face him, the one without the rifle, pivoting backwards as I did—six inches, maybe a foot closer to the road. The road was about fifteen feet away, maybe less. I didn't think looking to check the distance would help my cause. "I am staying here. In front of the bench."

"You are too far."

"No, I am not going anywhere. There is nowhere to go. I am waiting for the soldiers to come back from the school. I am, you see, a teacher in the school." I could hear the car. It was coming from the south.

"You are too far. Come back here."

"I will smoke a cigarette, then sit down with you." That didn't make any sense, but I could hear the car. I could see the car now, through the trees. I think the soldiers were mostly afraid of getting into trouble.

The soldiers walked over to me, one on each side. The rifle was now held in two hands, with the soldier facing me, facing the direction I wanted to run in, which made running a really poor gamble. "Look," I said, "let me go across the road and buy some cigarettes."

"No," he said, firmly. "You have to sit down."

I heard the car pass behind me and then it no longer made sense to be standing here, pissing off the soldiers. We all went back to the bench.

The other soldiers had been in the school for at least twenty minutes. One of the teachers came out and told me they were tearing the school apart. They were ransacking the student dormitories and the faculty housing. All the teachers had to leave, he said. The students were gathered in the cafeteria.

"Did you tell them I was a Peace Corps teacher?"

He shrugged. "What did you do, Mr. John? They are really mad at you and now we are all in trouble."

The teacher got in a brief, sharp exchange with the soldiers, which I couldn't follow, then they told him to leave. "Get out of here! Get out of here!"

Shit, I thought, not good.

There was, I knew, a shortcut to town. I had taken it once when I had missed the bus. Directly behind me was a large field, plowed, but dormant. On the far side of it was the slaughterhouse, a disgusting place full of dead and half-dead cattle. In between were irrigation ditches. Irrigation ditches in Afghanistan are quite deep, at least three feet, maybe two or three feet, wide.

The soldier held the rifle loosely in his left hand and I was thinking that I could ram my elbow into his face as I stood to grab the rifle, then smash the rifle butt into the face of the man on my right. They sat, two teenage draftees, staring vacantly forward, unaware that I held their lives in my hands. Then, I could hit them both a few more times in the head, run to the ditches, make it across the field to the slaughterhouse. Once in the slaughter house, I'd be out of anyone's line of fire, and once past the slaughterhouse, I'd be in the warren of streets and side streets that is Kabul. I could make it to the Embassy or to someone's house. Anyone's house. I could be somewhere besides here.

Then it occurred to me: this wasn't a James Bond movie. That was why I didn't have a trick cigarette that shot curare-tipped darts and why my belt buckle could not be converted into a helicopter. My muscles relaxed, I let out the air I had been packing into my lungs as I got ready to move. I'd wait for the soldiers to get back from the school. Either they would have realized their mistake or someone with a brain would have entered the picture, and I'd be able to go home.

I reached into my right pocket to get some matches so that I could smoke my last cigarette. My knuckles scraped the handle of the bayonet carried in a scabbard by the soldier on my right. Ah, I thought, showing them the matches and then lighting my cigarette, I can put the matches back in my pocket, grab the bayonet, stab the man with the rifle, then the man without the rifle. Then I could run to the ditches, etc. This seemed good. I turned it over in my mind as I turned the box of matches over in my fingers, over and over, letting them know I had not yet put it away. It seemed like a good idea. I slowly moved my feet under me, the better to spring forward: I'd finish the cigarette, absent-mindedly note that I still had the matches, go to put them away . . . Yes. A good plan.

I had to picture it. It was a rigid scabbard, so pulling it out with one hand wouldn't be difficult. Spin away from the man whose knife it was and stab it into the throat of the soldier with the rifle. That would be the tricky part because I had only one shot at that guy before having to deal with the man on my right. It has to be one-two, like clockwork, then into the ditches. I thought it could work.

Two more drags left on the cigarette. Feet in position, ready to shove off, spin, stab, turn, stab, run. Ready? Yes, ready. One more drag and then . . . Ah, yes, I am the English teacher. This is not a movie. Calm down. You're beginning to panic. I took the last drag of the cigarette and flicked it toward the road. I closed my eyes and leaned back on the bench. I concentrated on the play of light on my eyelids as the sun made its way through the leaves of the trees.

Time slowed down and then stopped. There are very few trees in Afghanistan. Except for the Soviet reforestation project at the base of the Kabul Gorge, I think there were seventeen trees in Afghanistan. Okay, maybe a few more. So it was nice sitting under these skinny, dirty little trees with my eyes closed and the soldiers part of someone else's strange tale of adventure. I had once tried showing photographs of Giant Sequoias to my students in the north and they thought I was playing a trick on them. Afghans are not used to symbolic three-dimensions and so have trouble interpreting photographs. All trees look like that, Mr. John, if you are really close to them. I could hear a faint breeze rustling the leaves. In Afghanistan you can hear everything because there are no competing sounds and the air is clear and thin.

Then the officer and the soldiers came back, and time clicked back into gear.

I was told to stand. I did, and walked over to the officer. My two soldiers were at my side, and four or five additional soldiers arced around the officer, facing me.

"You see," I said, "I am a teacher. I am in the American Peace Corps."

The officer punched me in the chest and shouted, spittle flying in the dusty mid-afternoon sun, "You are a spy! You are a member of the C.I.D.!"

I wanted to kill the little shit. You have to understand that being a teacher in an Islamic country provides a great deal of status. Being a foreigner provides additional status. Also, having seen grown Afghans fight with all the skill and force of American grammar school students, and being at least three or four inches taller than anyone in sight meant I simply wasn't going to take this nonsense. Plus, you have to realize, Afghanistan was a peaceful country. People simply did not push each other around. Because of all of this, the officer's inept punch was insulting. It was culturally shocking. And I was going to lay out the little fuck, knock him right on his ass—his nose would then best be described as the flat, red part of his face—but when I took a step forward, the soldiers facing me raised their rifles. And I stopped. I unclenched my fists.

It was then that it became really clear to me. It became absolutely obvious to me, standing there on the high plain of Afghanistan, in the quiet of the early afternoon, like a moment of enlightenment in which there is such perfect understanding of cause and effect—of consequences—that the past, present, and future all collapse into the transparent present: I should have taken the bayonet and stabbed the one with the rifle in the throat. I should have killed them both and run for the ditches.

It really had been a good plan.

STILL NOT ARRESTED

THE SOLDIERS WERE CARRYING BOXES OUT OF THE SCHOOL. A truck, maybe two, I forget, pulled up and a jeep was right behind them. I had been left alone with one soldier, who stood about four feet away from me with his rifle on his shoulder, aimed at my chest. I wanted to kick his ass, too, but he was way down the list so I let him alone.

When the jeep stopped, the officer came back from supervising the loading of the trucks. We are going to the Ministry of Defense, he told me. He got into the jeep first, sliding across the back seat so there would be room for me. The soldier with the rifle gestured me into the jeep and then got into the front seat, riding shotgun. That struck me as stupid. There was no way he could turn around and shoot me with his rifle in any sort of timely manner. I guessed that officers simply did not ride in the front no matter how rational that might be.

I had never been to the Ministry of Defense, but I knew where it was. There was an open plaza formed by the Ministry of Defense, the Ministry of the Interior, and the Presidential Palace. All were Victorian-style buildings, constructed during the brief time that England thought it could include Afghanistan in its Colonial empire. I also knew that in order to get there from here, it was necessary to drive past the U.S. Embassy. Knowing this, I held the lever up when I closed the door so that it wasn't actually latched. I held it tight against my leg so that it wouldn't bang on the bumps.

I had formulated another plan. I would, I thought, roll out of the jeep as we passed the Embassy and run like a maniac in the hope that I would be behind all those Marines by the time the jeep stopped and the soldier got out of the front seat. This plan would not be cast aside by thoughts of James Bond. James Bond was bullshit: I was in serious trouble and there were no half-naked women around to help me out of it.

We didn't talk, the four of us in the jeep. That was good. I concentrated on keeping the door tight against my leg and trying to remember exactly what the Embassy looked like. A fence out front, I knew, with a gate. Marines guarding the gate. We would make a left turn, I thought, and go past it almost immediately. So we wouldn't be traveling much more than twenty-five or thirty miles an hour. I'd gone off motorcycles at much higher speeds than that without breaking anything, so I should be okay, and even if I were hurt, I'd only have to run ten or twenty feet. Just enough to have the Marines able to cover me. I would have to roll, but not roll so far that I would end up in the ditch beside the road. As soon as I saw the Marines, I'd fall against the door and roll out of the jeep. I moved my feet back against the base of the seat so that I could push off and clear the back wheel.

But it didn't happen.

We made the turn and cruised past the Embassy that was guarded not by U.S. Marines, but by a contingent of Afghan soldiers. There were no Marines in sight. The Afghans straightened up and saluted as we went past and I let the door handle down so that the door was latched. My only hope now was that there would be a man with a brain at the end of this ride.

———

The plaza formed by the government buildings was a mess. There were tanks, armored personnel carriers, and sandbagged machine gun nests scattered all over in a huge, aggressive clutter. The jeep pulled up in front of the Ministry of Defense and the of-

ficer and the man with the rifle got out. The officer went into the
building while the soldier stood facing me. I didn't move.

What I expected was someone to come out and offer profuse
apologies: We are so sorry! This is such a grievous error! Please,
let us give you a ride home. The soldiers simply didn't understand
that you are an American Peace Corps volunteer, dedicated to the
practice of goodness. Again, please accept my apologies. I kept
myself busy with this fantasy. Perhaps they would replace my bicycle, which was, after all, the reason all this happened. As a gesture, you understand. Please, Mr. John, take *my* bicycle. We need
to prevent these situations from occurring again. One of those
new Chinese bikes with the metal linkage for the brakes. Oh, no,
that would be too much, I would say; well, all right, in the interest
of reconciliation.

But nothing was going well today.

He was big for an Afghan. Not tall, but broad, like a linebacker. Of course, my perspective was colored by the fact that
no one weighed anything in this country. He had lots of metal
on his shoulders, but I didn't know Afghan military ranks. I was
thinking colonel or major, something like that; the officer from
the tank being a lieutenant or captain, and this man obviously
of superior rank. The tank officer hung in the background. The
linebacker pulled open the door.

"Where did you get these photographs?" He waved the little
film strip in front of me. Five photographs, as if the King had
gone to a carnival and the Queen had said, "Hey, honey! A photo
booth!"

This was not a good beginning, but I wanted to be cooperative. There was, after all, the question of the bicycle. "I am glad
you asked so that we can get this straightened out," I said. "The
first time I saw them was when this man showed them to me." I
pointed to the tank officer.

"No, where did you get the photographs?"

There was a bit of a language problem here, I thought. My
Farsi was not going to be up to this, so I kept it simple.

"I didn't get the photographs. He had the photographs."

"You were seen dropping them in the bazaar."

"It must be a mistake. I did not have the photographs."

"You're a member of the C.I.D. We know this."

"I am in the Peace Corps. I am a teacher."

He had been leaning into the jeep, his right hand on the door, and now he stood up. Some time went past. Ten seconds, three minutes, something like that. Then he opened the door wider and leaned down and punched me in the chest. He grabbed me by my arm, pulled me out of the jeep, and pushed me toward the gate. I had a brief vision: running through the ditches to the slaughter-house. It really had been a good plan.

When the tank officer hit me, it had been a sissy punch and it had looked like a sissy punch. When this guy hit me, it looked like a real punch—a short, straight jab, good shoulder turn—but it had no force in it. I thought about this the rest of the day and into the early evening, not having very many complex things to consider. Partially, I attributed the lack of force to the awkward angle at which he was standing. But the physical impact of the blow was completely overwhelmed by its social impact. It wasn't that I was standing in a bar in San Francisco and some yo-yo punched me. I had been struck by a member of a foreign government who was acting in an official capacity. That was the major impact of being hit. It was as if I could hear doors closing.

They pushed me along. They pushed me down the walk, through the gate, across the little yard, up the steps, through the large lobby—not crowded, but a fair number of people turning to see this man, this criminal, they had caught trying to overthrow the government—then down the stairs and into a little room: pushed all the way, kept off balance. A few times it was the barrel of the rifle, but mostly it was the linebacker, pushing me high on my back, shoving me forward and spinning me at the same time. I remember it as being absolutely silent, but that was probably because I was thinking as fast as I could. I was trying to plan and the external world right now was of no significance and so I must have simply shut it out.

It was a little room, designed by Graham Greene: bare painted walls peeling and repainted, a threadbare sofa along the length of the narrow room, linoleum floor, a small desk, and behind it, I think, a chair. There were four people; later there would be five. The fifth one was a Soviet who stayed briefly, watching without saying anything, then left. I really only remember two: the linebacker and the old man. The Bad Cop and the Good Cop. It was as if I had tunnel vision. Only these two mattered, but I was aware of other people in the room: unfocused, silent. I can't even remember if the old man was in uniform or not, but my impression of him was never of a soldier. What he was wearing had no significance.

The pushing stopped and I turned to face the colonel.

"You will tell us," he said, "where you got the photographs."

"Look," I said. "I know nothing of any photographs."

"You are lying. You will tell us."

"You have convinced me that you are serious about this," I said. "If I had anything to tell you, I would tell you."

He laughed and looked at the other people in the room. "We are serious. You will tell us and we will kill you. We will shoot you this evening."

My brain, you have to understand, was moving at something approaching the speed of light. It was close to being an out-of-body experience: I was watching—witnessing, almost—and analyzing and planning because there had to be a way out of this. I remember thinking that these people were really inept. If you are going to kill me anyway, then what is my motivation for talking? This must be straight out of the manual that states a prisoner should sit behind the man in the jeep who is ostensibly guarding him.

He threw another punch that hit me in the chest and knocked me back onto the sofa. Like all the punches today, I knew that it happened, but whatever pain it could have caused was dismissed by my scheming mind as irrelevant. Eventually, I guess they must have hit me fifty times. Something like that. But I have no memory that they ever hurt me. In retrospect, I think that must have freaked them out somewhat.

Of course, as I mentioned, Afghans are not good fighters. This must sound so absurd now, in light of the twenty years of violence and war that have destroyed that country. But this was still in the beginning when, for all their warrior mythology, Afghans were an extraordinarily non-violent people. For instance, they kept hitting me in the chest as I stood with my calves against the front of the sofa. They'd hit me, and I would fall back on to the sofa. It became a ritual, so after a while I would start to fall before they actually hit me and they never appeared to notice.

I had an almost overwhelming desire to teach them how to do this. Hadn't they ever seen a movie? First, they should have taken off my glasses, because it is really hard to be a tough guy when you can't see shit. A blurry world is a scary world. Second, get over this grade-school phobia and hit me in the face. Nothing like a bloody nose, split lip, or a swelling eye to make one rethink things. Hit me in the stomach. Why are you hitting me in the best protected part of my body? I felt like Br'er Rabbit, "Oh, please, Mr. Colonel, please don't hit me in the chest where I am covered by ribs and muscle."

And, for pity's sake: it's the CIA, not the CID!

We got into a routine:

"Stand up!"

I'd stand up.

"Where did you get the photographs?"

"I don't have any photographs."

He'd punch me in the chest. I'd fall on the sofa.

"Stand up!"

I'd stand up.

"Tell me the names of the Afghans you know."

"I don't know any Afghans."

He'd punch me in the chest. I'd fall on the sofa.

"Stand up!"

I'd stand up.

"Who do you work for?"

"I work for the Peace Corps."

He'd punch me in the chest. I'd fall on the sofa.

"Stand up!"

I'd stand up. I would say, "I want to call my Embassy."

He'd punch me in the chest. I'd fall on the sofa.

"Stand up!"

I'd stand up and we would start again.

This lasted for a couple of hours. Then they all left.

Since I was sitting on the sofa, I remained sitting. It occurred to me that I could try to sneak out of the building, but then I thought my getaway would be dependent on that bicycle I thought they were going to give me. Since that didn't seem likely, I just rested. They were gone for about half an hour.

They all piled back in. The Soviet was with them. The linebacker sat facing me, one hip on the corner of the desk. He lit a cigarette. The old man sat right beside me, on my right. Someone was on my left, but he didn't matter. Tunnel vision.

The old man said, "We really have to know about the photographs."

This again. "I never saw them before the soldiers showed them to me."

"So you say." He turned to face me. He pointed to my crotch. "We have electricity, you know." He had a kind face and a gentle, reasonable way of speaking, even when he was talking about plugging my balls into the wall socket.

"Yes," I told him. "This is a very modern country. The United States, I think, built the generator."

He ignored that. "Just tell us who you work for."

"I work for the Peace Corps. I am a teacher."

He shook his head. "You have been very well trained. You always say the same thing."

"I was trained as an English teacher. I say the same thing because it is true."

"Tell us where you live. We want to search your house."

Ah, finally. I'd been hoping for this one. I drew a map to the house of the U.S. Ambassador. They all left the room. About half an hour later they came back and yelled at me: You don't live there. Where do you really live?

I insisted. It was temporary, I said, but that's where I lived. They yelled some more. Tell us where you really live.

What I did next is difficult to explain. I thought about giving the address of the Peace Corps nurse, because her husband is a member of the Embassy staff. I had to let someone know where I was. But Kay had two children, so that seemed like an irresponsible thing to do, to send soldiers to search their house. Somehow, I had to let someone know where I was. Then it occurred to me. I thought about this at light speed, turning it over and over, knowing it was bad, but wondering if it were forgivable. I would tell them where Chuck Norton lived. Let them search Chuck's house.

Norton was the only person I knew, that I have ever known, who would not go through the this-isn't-a-movie second guessing. Norton would know instantly that something was very bad and he would know how to act. I really didn't think a couple of Afghan soldiers were any match for Chuck. And if none of this worked out, if they ended up killing us both, I thought he would, at the very least, understand that he had been my only hope. I have known a few people I would trust with my life, without hesitation or second thoughts, but Chuck was the only one who would understand immediately that if soldiers showed up knowing his name, wanting to search "my room," he would have to get out. Get away. Both know this and be able to actually do it. Chuck Norton. An amazing guy.

The linebacker smoked cigarettes and fidgeted. He glared at me periodically. We were in some sort of limbo stage. People left, other people came in. The old man left, then returned to his seat beside me. They were waiting for something. I was wondering if my map to Chuck's house was at all readable. I had made it deliberately vague. They would drive around all night trying to make sense of my map or they would make the right assumptions and find Chuck. They'd search the house, making lots of noise, asserting themselves, and at some point they'd notice that Chuck was no longer there. Then they would look for him, afraid to report back with notice of any sort of screw-up. Chuck would get to someone who could get to the ambassador. Time would go by. It did. We all waited.

The linebacker was the first to break. He stood up. Lit another cigarette. He paced back and forth in the tiny space between the desk and the wall to my right. We all watched him. He threw the cigarette on the ground.

"Who do you work for?" he yelled. "Tell me who you work for!"

I started to say that I worked for the Peace Corps, but he was busy fumbling at his holster, drawing his little pistol. It was an automatic. Maybe a thirty-eight. It looked small. He jammed it into my forehead. "Tell me now! I am going to kill you now unless you tell me."

I tried to think of what to say. I can still feel it today, the barrel against my forehead. There was nothing left to say. All the words had been used already and none had worked. I remember thinking that I was about to be killed by a band of very stupid people, and that struck me as grossly unfair. "Then shoot me now," I finally said, "because I have nothing to tell you."

And I waited. I remember actually leaning into the gun, resting against it. My eyes were closed and I waited. And then the gun was gone and everyone left the room.

AT LONG LAST, NOT ARRESTED AT ALL

I LEANED BACK IN THE SOFA, LETTING MY HEAD LOLL AGAINST the cushions. I emptied my mind of any thoughts. The soldiers were gone fifteen or twenty minutes this time. Once in a while, as I sat there—eyes closed, breathing slowly—I could feel ideas and concerns trying to creep in to my consciousness. Each time, I gently pushed them back. There was no future in my life, there was only whatever was happening at the moment and, right now, nothing was happening, so planning, worrying, figuring, calculating—all had absolutely no value. I would simply end up creating a picture that I would have to change as soon as the circus started again.

They weren't giving up on this idea that I was a spy. And, according to all the rumors, there were executions taking place nightly. My only hope, I thought, was Chuck, and that was a slim one. So, I just emptied my mind and rested.

Years later, I told this story to John Gagnon, a sociologist in New York. He, in turn, told me a story of being on a bus in rural Africa that was stopped and boarded by a squad of soldiers. The soldiers acted like thugs, he said, lazy, contemptuous and powerful in the close confines of the small bus. Gagnon understood then how thin the structure of civility was, how loosely attached to the human condition, and that all those concerns we had as intellectuals and academics—rationality, evidence, logic, justice, history—had almost no foothold on the bus at all . . . a language spoken on a distant planet. On the bus, there were a few men sweating in their cheap uniforms, brandishing their hand-me-down weapons, who could kill him or humiliate him or leave him completely alone, depending on how they felt at the moment.

It wasn't that these Afghans who had taken me were stupid. It was that their concerns were completely unrelated to mine, and mine didn't matter. I thought of Afghanistan as a place on the map—a splotch of orange, perhaps—at the bottom of Asia, and Asia the huge tail on the small dog that was Europe. I could almost feel the enormous weight of the Soviet Union pressing down on us, and I longed for the oceans the Afghans never saw, but that I could almost hear when I went to sleep at night. I think these men saw Afghanistan itself and it was a more complex place than I knew, factioned and dug in, splintered by ridges and ravines, and by history, family, ethnicity and language. I think these men were thinking about Kandahar and Bamiyan, wondering if Herat would hold, and wishing the soldier hadn't shot that mullah in Ghazni.

In concrete terms, I was without consequence. No one really knew how many people had been killed in the last week, so one more wouldn't matter very much. And, as my student had said, once you start killing people, it doesn't matter which people you decide to kill. However, if one fantasized for a moment, I could be seen as a threat of considerable proportions. It was because of this contrast that they kept leaving and coming back to me. Or so I thought in the weeks that followed. I had told them earlier that killing me was also killing a great deal of foreign aid, but that caused them no apparent concern: as Communists, their new government leaders had probably already written off that source of revenue. The years of balancing between the U.S. and Soviet blocs were over, so no aid from America was expected. But what if this obvious bumbler, this dropper-of-photographs, was actually part of an American reactionary force? That would be something to worry about.

It must have been something along these lines, or they just would have tossed me in the prison or had me shot. They really wanted to know exactly what sort of a pain in the ass I was. One thing I felt pretty sure about: I was a practical problem for them, not a moral one. Morality had nothing to do with this room. This room was John Gagnon's bus, and I was just along for the ride.

They came back in and I sat up. It wouldn't do to appear too relaxed. The man who wanted to shoot me hung back somewhat, while Mr. Electricity came over to talk to me.

"There's been a mistake," he said.

I thought, no shit. I said, "Oh?"

"Yes, a mistake. We would like you to come upstairs with us."

"Can I call my embassy?" This was a test.

"We will take care of all of that," he told me, unaware he had just failed an exam. "Now we should go upstairs."

I thought about refusing. They all watched me think it over. I would have understood if they had picked me up by the scruff of my neck and thrown me out in the street, dusting their hands like satisfied cartoon characters. I didn't understand why they admitted making a mistake. But staying here made no sense, so I got up. No one hit me. The little gun stayed in the holster.

Mr. Electricity said, "Good. We will all go up together."

"Sure," I said, and we all went trooping out the door, down the short hallway, and up the stairs to the lobby.

There were five or six in my entourage and there were a few dozen younger officers milling about the lobby, staring at us as we crossed.

"We will eat," I was told and we went into a room that looked like an officer's mess. That explained all the soldiers in the lobby: they had been kicked out of their dining room. We sat in the middle of one of the long narrow tables. The colonel sat directly across from me. Mr. Electricity sat on my right. The other people didn't matter.

"We are sorry about the mistake," said the colonel. He looked like he wanted to kill me. This was a performance, but I couldn't identify the audience. The other men who were with the three of us didn't seem to be in positions of authority, although they were watching the charade very carefully.

"These are confusing times," I told the colonel. "It's easy to make mistakes."

We sat in silence for a few minutes, then Mr. Electricity asked me if I wanted some water from the pitcher in the middle of the table. I told him I wasn't thirsty. He poured himself a tall glass and the sound of the splashing water was wonderful, but I really doubted these people boiled the water for twenty minutes in order to kill the invisible bugs. The food finally came and we all picked up our spoons and started eating. It was good. It was like the food they had served at the bank.

"This is good," I told them.

Mr. Electricity leaned toward me. "Now that this is over," he said, "and we are eating like friends, there is just one thing I would like to understand."

"What is that?" I asked him.

He put his hand on my forearm, a gesture of friendship. "Well, I would like to know where you got the photographs."

I looked across the table at the colonel. He was staring at me, spoon suspended midway to his mouth. It was all a trick, this little dining experience. They had spoken with someone, or Mr. Electricity had convinced them that the rough stuff wasn't working and they needed to try something subtler. Someone, at any rate, had said, "Let's get him to let down his guard. Let's tell him it's all over." And then they had concocted this dinner scenario.

I tried to say something, but my mouth was too dry. I swallowed a few times, then said, "You know, I will have some of that water after all."

He filled my glass. I drank it all and held it out to be refilled. I drank about half of the second glass. "It is as I've told you," I said. "I first saw the photographs when the officer showed them to me. The question you need to ask is where he got them."

He shook his head in mock admiration. "You are so well trained."

"Peace Corps training is very good," I said. "I am an English teacher."

"Of course," he said. "But we are running out of time. I think we have finished eating."

I had drunk the water because I figured they would kill me before I had time to get sick. Later, in a meeting, another volunteer said to me, "I don't believe you really thought they were going to kill you." It was an odd remark and I wasn't sure how to respond. After thinking for a minute, I said that I had been offered water and drunk it, and then everyone in the room knew that I had expected to die.

We all got up from the table and left the dining room. We went through the front doors of the building and stood on the porch that ran the width of the building, looking out over the debris of revolutions. There were two or three steps down to the small fenced yard and then another dozen steps to the guarded gate. Through the gate, was the plaza, jammed with military equipment: tanks, machine-gun nests, anti-aircraft weapons and a motley collection of jeeps, trucks, cars, and armored vehicles. We stood on the porch surveying all of this. The colonel lit a cigarette.

"You can go," he said to me, with a small gesture indicating that I go down the stairs, across the yard, and through the gate. Standing there, I could still feel his eyes on me as when, back in the dining room, Mr. Electricity had asked me where I had gotten the photographs. This was the solution, I thought: shot while trying to escape. The method of killing me would justify the killing of me, confirming my nefarious nature. That would be the end of it, a sodden bit of garbage left by America on Afghanistan's front stoop, to be scooped up by the Embassy and sent back to the United States.

Years before, as a college student working the graveyard shift in a motel, I had been robbed at gunpoint. After taking the money, the robber had waved his pistol at me and told me to get down on the floor. I told him I wouldn't do it and he had gotten excited, waving the gun more emphatically as if I had not seen it. This is what I'll do, I told him, I'll squat down and lean against the counter here so that I can't see you leave, but I am not lying down on the floor. He thought it over, nodded a few times, and then ran out as I slid below the level of the counter. I had a real thing about being shot in the back. I wanted to see the people who killed me; it was an attitude that had gotten me in some trouble in the Army.

"I think we should call my embassy," I said to the colonel.

"You need to go now. Your people are waiting for you."

I looked and saw no one but Afghan soldiers. "Let's all go out together," I suggested.

"No," he said. "You go by yourself." He pushed me and I stumbled down the steps.

I turned to look at him, standing above me, and thought it would be humiliating to scramble back up on the porch. I remembered an old psychology professor who had told us that humans were the only animals willing to risk death rather than embarrassment. I walked across the yard, toward the soldier at the gate who—at the last possible moment it seemed to me—stepped out of my way to let me through. There was a tank or an armored personnel carrier immediately in front of me and, as I looked around in the last faint light of evening, I could see no one who could be considered to be on my side. I just kept walking. They would either let me keep walking or they would shoot me. I walked past the front of the tank and there, minuscule and in some bright, completely incongruous color, was a Volkswagen beetle, and next to it a heavyset American.

"Are you John Sumser?" he asked, offering his hand.

"Yes, I am."

"I'm here to get you out of here."

Norton is behind this, I thought, and then suddenly the circus clowns were back: the linebacker, Mr. Electricity, and the rest of my dinner companions. The Embassy guy spoke with them, shaking hands with each of them. The colonel then turned to me and offered me his hand.

"Oh, go fuck yourself," I told him.

The Embassy guy listed toward me, the great ship of state rolling with the tide. He was still facing the Afghans, smiling at them, and said softly out of the side of his mouth, "Look around you. Do you think we have any chance of getting out of here if they don't want us to?"

It was a good point. Its Nazi origins not withstanding, VW beetles were not geared for combat. I shook the hands of each of the men. I thanked Mr. Electricity for dinner.

And then we left.

Someone pushed a drink into my hand, the glass wet with condensation, and I held it as if it were a stone or a book. "Drink it," someone said, and so I did. Whiskey and seven-up, with ice-cubes bumping against my lip. It tasted like all of America, like bowling alleys or baseball on spring mornings.

I was sitting on a sofa. There was a woman on one side of me, and a man who asked me questions in the most considerate way imaginable. It was like an out-of-body experience. The man from the Embassy had whisked me away in his little VW and deposited me here, at an Embassy cocktail party. Scotty had finally figured out how to get the lithium crystals back to full strength and I had been beamed back on board the Enterprise.

I had asked him, as we drove, "Did Chuck Norton get ahold of you? Is he okay?"

"Who's Chuck Norton?"

The story the Embassy man told me was that a man from another ministry had asked what all the commotion was about and, on being told an American spy had been captured, had contacted his superiors, who had phoned the Embassy. "It's the highest level contact we've had since the coup," the man from the Embassy had said. Something, then, to be proud of. And Chuck was not in the picture at all.

I had told the story in the VW and told it again at the party. Someone had asked me what I had learned or what I felt, now that it was over. I said that I should have tried to make a run for it when we had driven past the U.S. Embassy.

The man with the VW said, "Then I would have been called to identify your body rather than giving you a ride home."

"Yes, but that could have happened anyway," I said. "And when he had that gun against my head, my regret was that I hadn't tried."

After a while, they pushed a mostly full liter bottle of Canadian Club into my hands and gave me a ride back to my apartment. I met another volunteer, but for the life of me, I cannot remember who it was. Probably one of the guys from upstairs. We walked around the neighborhood, talking and drinking the Canadian Club. We ended up sitting on the curb on the corner, and an Afghan who ran the little shop there came out and asked us for some of the whiskey. I almost poured him some, but when I looked at the other volunteer, he shook his head and so I told the Afghan that I couldn't give him any.

We were Peace Corps volunteers, after all, and were not there to corrupt the natives.

After that, I wandered back to my place and went to sleep.

AFTERWARD

"You should talk with the other volunteers," the director told me the following day. "They should hear what happened."

Since the coup, a lot of volunteers had taken to hanging out in the Peace Corps offices, so spreading the word about a meeting was easier than it would have been a month earlier. I told the director that I would hang around until he could organize something, then I turned to go down the hall to Kay's office. Kay would already know what had happened because her husband was at the Embassy. Before I could move away, the director called my name and I turned around.

"I haven't seen Norton today," he said to me. "I assume he's all right?"

All the air went out of the room and my heart started racing. I had forgotten about Chuck. I had thought since the Embassy guy in the VW didn't know about Chuck, that nothing had happened to him.

"What about Norton? Why wouldn't he be all right?" I asked, keeping my voice as normal as I could.

Now the director was confused. "Wasn't he with you?"

"No. Why would you think that?"

"The man from the Embassy said that they were told two Americans had been picked up." The director stared at me as if he was worried about my mental health. "Two Americans: you and Norton."

"Oh, shit."

"You didn't know this?"

"No, but I know what it's about. I think it's a mistake. Look, I'll find Chuck. I'll get back to you."

"I think you should get some sleep. Go home. Come back around eleven and we'll have a meeting."

I shook my head. "No, I'm fine. I need to find out about Chuck."

I didn't actually run to Kay's office, but only because I wasn't sure I could control my muscles. Not only that: if I panicked, it would mean that I really believed that I had gotten Chuck arrested and I desperately didn't want to believe that. So I pretended not to panic—which is nowhere near the same thing as being calm—and thought about Chuck sitting on the sofa in some basement room while I wandered around Kabul with a bottle of Canadian Club. So I didn't actually run nor did I scream in anger or cry out in frustration and remorse. I just walked, stiff-legged, down the hall to Kay's office.

Kay wanted to know if I was all right.

"Oh, yeah, sure," I told her, my heart a cold spasm in my chest. "I'm fine. Did you see Chuck last night?"

"No. Yesterday afternoon," she said. "You really ought to go to the Embassy and have the doctor look at you."

"I'm fine, Kay." I'm dead, I thought. Even last night in the basement, sending them to Norton's house seemed questionable. In the bright light of this new morning, it seemed incomprehensible. "They really can't hit very hard and they just punched me in the chest."

"Let me see."

I opened my shirt and let her look at my chest. Thin, white, lower ribs showing: just like always. "I'm fine, Kay, but I really have to talk with Chuck. If you see him before I do, tell him he has to talk with me first."

"What's wrong, John?"

"Was Chuck arrested?"

"Chuck? No. It was just you."

"The director thinks Chuck was picked up as well."

She shook her head emphatically. She and Chuck were good friends, so she didn't want to hear this either. "Larry would have told me. It was just you."

"Could you call him? Larry?" Her husband should know what was going on.

She said she would and I walked outside and sat on the steps. I lit a cigarette, thinking about what I would do if they had grabbed Chuck. Thinking about what I would do if they hadn't. I spent the next hour or so thinking about this, wandering the halls in search of my soul. At one point Kay interrupted my pacing long enough to tell me that her husband had reaffirmed that Norton, as far as he knew, had never been picked up. The only part that stayed in my brain longer than a second or two was "as far as he knew." Then, coming out of the library a half hour later, I saw Chuck walking down the hall toward me, past the mailboxes.

"Kay told me what happened," he said. "You okay?"

"Yeah, but I have to tell you something." So I gave it to him fast, in a low voice, standing there in the hallway with the light flooding in through the long row of windows. Just the downtown part: questions, punching, questions, punching, gun in forehead, then where do you live? Where do you live? And giving them the ambassador's house, then giving them Chuck's house. I remember touching him on the chest, leaning forward. "I racked my brain, Chuck. You were it. You were the only person in this country I thought could do me some good, who would know what to do when the soldiers came."

Chuck was just staring at me, lightly balanced but unmovable in that boxer's stance he had. We were standing very close together. He didn't say anything. I said, "You were the only person I thought would understand if it didn't work out." Didn't work out, a euphemism for if you got killed. He nodded. Chuck understood euphemisms.

"I need to know," I said, "if we're okay on this."

Maybe this was the third miracle in Afghanistan, I'm not sure.

"Of course," he said without any hesitation. "I would have done the same thing."

I told the story again to the volunteers gathered in the library. I convinced the skeptics by telling them about drinking the water. One person asked if I thought I had been singled out because I had long hair.

"I don't have long hair," I said and everyone laughed. My hair was halfway down my back, but I just thought that I was in need of a haircut, not that I was a long-haired person. I hadn't had a haircut in about eighteen months, mostly because the women volunteers who acted as the unofficial barbers were never around during my brief forays into the capital. "Okay, my hair is a little long," I said when they stopped laughing. "But I don't think that was it. I think it was just bad luck, because it all hinges on the motivation of the officer who accused me of dropping the pictures. Everyone's actions make sense but his, and he just happened to be stationed by my school instead of someone else's."

"I want to say something," Marty said. Marty was leaning against the wall. He had been avoiding me all morning. Marty had been acting vaguely hostile ever since Mahmood had kissed me in front of him.

"Sure, Marty."

"You have to stop saying you were arrested. You weren't arrested."

"Oh." I had no idea what point he was trying to make. "You mean that arrested isn't the right word or that none of this happened?"

"Something happened, but you weren't arrested. You didn't go to trial, for example."

This was too strange an argument for me to follow, so I just told him to think up an appropriate word that we could use to label what had happened.

"Whatever the word is," he said smugly, "it isn't arrested."

Chuck later told me that Marty was jealous. Marty wanted to be the one picked up and interrogated. Marty, as far as most volunteers were concerned, was a spy. Chuck thought it really bothered Marty that while he was the spy, it was I—the Afghan-kissing volunteer—who got the credit. And it didn't help that Chuck, who had never shown him any respect, had also been on the Afghan list of Americans who posed a threat to the new regime. Chuck thought that Marty wanted to be on that list.

"The credit?"

"I think that's how he sees it."

Chuck was probably right.

"Did you know he sleeps in a nightshirt?" I asked him. "Like the Night Before Christmas?"

"That's probably why the Afghans weren't worried about him."

The meeting was winding down. We talked about trying to keep tabs on each other so that if one of us went missing, someone else would notice. Then a volunteer asked me what I thought a person should do if he was picked up.

"This will sound bad," I said. My voice quavered slightly and I tried to stop it. "But if there is a good chance to run, you should run." I didn't know if I should continue, but then I blurted out, "If there is a good chance to get away if you can kill the person holding you, you should kill him."

"John!" the director said. "John, this is the Peace Corps. The Peace Corps."

"I know," I told him. Maybe I should have gone back home and taken a nap this morning because now I felt infinitely tired. "But it was my one regret when he said he was going to shoot me. I should have tried to get away. I kept thinking that I would meet a rational person, but there are no rational people in the middle of a coup. This isn't the United States. They can do anything they want." And then I knew Marty was right: I hadn't been arrested, because there was no law in effect. The country was being run with guns and quick impressions.

The Afghans were keeping loose tabs on me and Chuck. There was usually someone hanging around outside my place in the morning. When I left, I would be followed. They weren't much better at following than they were at interrogation, so they would frequently lose me. When this happened, the follower would either quit for the day or head back to my place, knowing that sooner or later I'd show up.

I did a lot of walking in the days following the meeting, because the Peace Corps had been told that I was no longer allowed to work in Afghanistan. I could stay, but I couldn't work. The director was trying to resolve this problem. He had offered me a job taking care of the library, but I couldn't imagine doing that for the rest of my time. (The library, though, was amazingly good given that it was created from all the books left behind by volunteers. Around the room, on top of the tall shelves, were large jars with equally large tapeworms floating inside. Sigourney Weaver would have felt right at home.)

I walked all over Kabul, aimlessly poking around in parts I had never known about. But tension was rising in the city. An Islamic leader had been killed in Ghazni while leading a protest against some of the educational reforms the new government was putting in place. It was widely, but still unofficially, recognized that the communists were the ones running the country. A U.S. information officer was shot and killed outside of the USAID office and we were all told to limit our movements to the extent we could.

One evening, I walked over to Chuck's house. I had been downtown, wandering in the smaller streets and had lost my follower from confusion or boredom. Streets in Kabul were lined by high walls with deeply inset gates leading to the front yards of the homes. When I turned into the alcove to ring the bell on Chuck's gate, I came face to face with an Afghan man who had been hiding there. He must have been waiting for Chuck to leave, thinking he would hear the house door and have plenty of time to move away from the gate.

I slammed him against the wall, yelling something at him. I don't remember what I was yelling, but he had startled me and

I wasn't going to let anyone take me back to that basement. I grabbed him by the shoulders and smashed him around the little alcove, then threw him out in the street, shouting at him: Get out of here! Get out of here! He ran down the street and disappeared around the corner.

I lit a cigarette and leaned against the wall, waiting for my heart rate to come back down. I stayed there for quite a while, smoking on the quiet street, hunched in my jacket against the cool night air, and thinking about what I had just done. Then I walked over to the director's house, surprising him because it was getting late and because I had never visited him before.

"Have a seat, John," he said. "Would you like something? Some tea?"

I told him I was fine, that I didn't need anything. We sat down in his living room. He had decorated the room with an interesting collection of artifacts. He was probably a man I should have gotten to know.

I told him what had happened in front of Chuck's house. "I think," I told him, "that it's time for me to leave Afghanistan."

"Then perhaps a beer," he said, and I agreed.